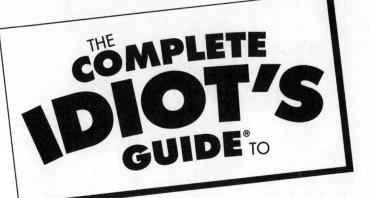

THE COMPLETE IDIOT'S GUIDE® TO

Motor Scooters

D1051899

*by Bev Brinson and
Bryce Ludwig*

A member of Penguin Group (USA) Inc.

ALPHA BOOKS

Published by the Penguin Group

Penguin Group (USA) Inc., 375 Hudson Street, New York, New York 10014, U.S.A.

Penguin Group (Canada), 10 Alcorn Avenue, Toronto, Ontario, Canada M4V 3B2 (a division of Pearson Penguin Canada Inc.)

Penguin Books Ltd, 80 Strand, London WC2R 0RL, England

Penguin Ireland, 25 St Stephen's Green, Dublin 2, Ireland (a division of Penguin Books Ltd)

Penguin Group (Australia), 250 Camberwell Road, Camberwell, Victoria 3124, Australia (a division of Pearson Australia Group Pty Ltd)

Penguin Books India Pvt Ltd, 11 Community Centre, Panchsheel Park, New Delhi—110 017, India

Penguin Group (NZ), cnr Airborne and Rosedale Roads, Albany, Auckland 1310, New Zealand (a division of Pearson New Zealand Ltd)

Penguin Books (South Africa) (Pty) Ltd, 24 Sturdee Avenue, Rosebank, Johannesburg 2196, South Africa

Penguin Books Ltd, Registered Offices: 80 Strand, London WC2R 0RL, England

International Standard Book Number: 978-1-59257-639-5
Library of Congress Catalog Card Number: 2006938602

09 08 07   8 7 6 5 4 3 2 1

Interpretation of the printing code: The rightmost number of the first series of numbers is the year of the book's printing; the rightmost number of the second series of numbers is the number of the book's printing. For example, a printing code of 07-1 shows that the first printing occurred in 2007.

Printed in the United States of America

Note: This publication contains the opinions and ideas of its authors. It is intended to provide helpful and informative material on the subject matter covered. It is sold with the understanding that the authors and publisher are not engaged in rendering professional services in the book. If the reader requires personal assistance or advice, a competent professional should be consulted.

The authors and publisher specifically disclaim any responsibility for any liability, loss, or risk, personal or otherwise, which is incurred as a consequence, directly or indirectly, of the use and application of any of the contents of this book.

Most Alpha books are available at special quantity discounts for bulk purchases for sales promotions, premiums, fund-raising, or educational use. Special books, or book excerpts, can also be created to fit specific needs.

For details, write: Special Markets, Alpha Books, 375 Hudson Street, New York, NY 10014.

Publisher: *Marie Butler-Knight*
Editorial Director: *Mike Sanders*
Managing Editor: *Billy Fields*
Acquisitions Editor: *Paul Dinas*
Development Editor: *Michael Thomas*
Production Editor: *Megan Douglass*

Copy Editor: *Jan Zoya*
Cover Designer: *Bill Thomas*
Book Designers: *Trina Wurst*
Indexer: *Brad Herriman*
Layout: *Ayanna Lacey*
Proofreader: *Aaron Black*

To my family and friends. I could have never taken a risk without each and every one of them. If I start naming names it would go on for pages. And to scooterists everywhere who have made this adventure so much fun and well worth all the work. Enjoy the ride. —Bev

Dedicated to my parents, Deb and Steve, for their patience and support. To my siblings Zach, Greg, and Emily, for shaping my character. And to all the scooterists who have encouraged me along the way. —Bryce

Contents at a Glance

Contents

Introduction

Complete idiots riding scooters? Perish the thought. It doesn't take
a rocket scientist to ride a scooter, but complete idiots operating
machinery of any kind does not seem prudent. Fortunately, you're not
a complete idiot. Picking up *The Complete Idiot's Guide to Motor Scooters*
demonstrates intelligence. You know how to find out more about a subject you have no prior knowledge of. Picking up this book also means
you have an interest in scooters, also a sign of someone who is at least a
bit brighter than the average bulb.

The hardest part of being new to scooters is where to get started.
Buying a new vehicle can be intimidating. Buying a type of vehicle you
know almost nothing about is even more so—particularly when you
don't have a friend or relative to turn to for advice on the subject. Not
knowing how to operate a scooter is another confidence killer. In this
book we try to remove as much of the mystery and fear as possible by
giving potential scooter owners a foundation to continue to build upon.
Beyond just knowing how to pick out a scooter or how to ride it, we
want you to feel confident about becoming a scooterist.

How to Use This Book

Roughly two thirds of this book is filled with useful information that
can be readily applied to anyone who buys a scooter. The rest of the
book may not be for everyone, but it does expand the horizons of
scooter owners who want to do more with their scooter than just commute on a fun and efficient vehicle.

Part 1, "The Scooter World," gives a broad overview of the history
of scooters and the significance of some particularly important models.
This section also covers the basic mechanical systems of scooters, and
how they work. Knowing why a scooter does what it does is really an
asset when it comes time to shop for a scooter. To find the right scooter
you have to be able to ask the right questions, take test rides, and do
your homework. Chapter 3 is a great guide to picking the right scooter
for your needs and wants.

Part 2, "What to Expect," covers the things you need to know about
actually owning a scooter. Basic riding tips are presented, along with

advice on where to go to get expert instruction on how to ride safely and proficiently. Maintenance needs of scooters are also detailed in this section, along with general explanations of procedures of most routine services to be performed on a scooter.

Part 3, "Fun Stuff," presents a range of scooter lifestyle stuff that is just for fun. Accessories, racing, events, scooter rallies, and the camaraderie of a scooter club are all things that are completely optional but really fun parts of owning a scooter. Scootering has a definite social component that many scooter owners find irresistible. In theory, riding alone should be every bit as good as riding in a group, but there is something about group riding that enhances the whole experience. It's all about enjoying your scooter on a whole new level.

Extras

Look for sidebars throughout the book for quick hints, warnings, interesting facts, and definitions of unfamiliar terminology.

Kick Start

These sidebars contain brief, helpful tips that supplement nearby parts of the chapter.

Scootrivia

Reading Scootrivia sidebars will make you look like less of a rookie the next time you find yourself hanging out with more seasoned scooter owners.

Oil Slick

These sidebars are there to warn you about potential hazards and perils.

def•i•ni•tion

You'll find definitions of unfamiliar words in these boxes and in the glossary in Appendix C.

Acknowledgments

There are too many people to list individually who have helped with *The Complete Idiot's Guide to Motor Scooters* and *ScooterWorld* magazine. There are manufacturers, distributors, accessory manufacturers, mechanics, racers, and scooter shops. Through the years, they have been so generous with their time, knowledge, and products. There are some wonderful individuals working in the field. Family and friends who listened to ideas, offered advice, packed boxes in the garage, stuffed envelopes, edited copy, created illustrations, wrote stories, and just listened. Writers who came forward to help with the magazine and have continued to contribute so much more than stories, they have become great friends. And scooterists who make it all so interesting and fun. I can't thank everyone enough.

When I announced to family and friends that we were going to write *The Complete Idiot's Guide to Motor Scooters*, the response was overwhelming. I had numerous volunteers for "test idiots" and offers to do anything to help. The ongoing enthusiasm and support made those late nights and weekends of work all worthwhile.

A special thank you to Bryce Ludwig. Without his dedicated hard work and many hours of writing, this book would not have been possible.

I lift a glass of Chianti and simply say to all a heartfelt, "grazie."

Bev Brinson
Publisher
ScooterWorld magazine

Trademarks

All terms mentioned in this book that are known to be or are suspected of being trademarks or service marks have been appropriately capitalized. Alpha Books and Penguin Group (USA) Inc. cannot attest to the accuracy of this information. Use of a term in this book should not be regarded as affecting the validity of any trademark or service mark.

Part 1

The Scooter World

Once you get a scooter, you are instantly in a "club." You'll immediately notice others on two-wheeled machines waving low and close to their side or nodding in a knowing fashion. They know what you will soon know—how much fun riding a scooter is, and how friendly the two-wheeled community is. You'll meet many other scooterists, motorcyclists, and curious people.

The history of scooters is rich, and the growing popularity illustrates what a viable mode of transportation scooters are. Enjoy!

Chapter 1

Scooter Design Through the Ages

In This Chapter

◆ The first scooter

◆ Scooters in America

◆ Unique designs

Scooters have a rich history that spans the globe, with major contributions from the United States. Throughout the past century, they have provided transportation and have given personal mobility to people in many parts of the world.

Scootering Around the World

There are few populated parts of the world where scooters are completely unknown. In parts of Asia they outnumber cars many times over. Though the scooter may have been born in France, it did much of its growing up in the U.S. After WWII it attended charm school in Italy and begat children all around the world.

The Auto-Fauteuil

In 1902, a French inventor came up with a set of features that came to broadly define scooters. The Auto-Fauteuil had a *step-through frame*. The engine was tucked away out of sight behind rudimentary bodywork. This earliest scooter was built for easy and comfortable riding. It laid the foundation for everything that followed.

Scootrivia
Fauteuil is a French term for an open-sided armchair.

def•i•ni•tion

Similar to a girl's bicycle, a **step-through frame** or body allows your leg to easily cross in front of you as you get on the bike instead of swinging it up, behind, and over.

Early Scooters in America

A number of small scooter firms came and went between 1902 and 1935. Some stuck with the formula established in the beginning, and others very closely resembled the modern stand-up "go-peds."

Salsbury introduced the Motor Glide in 1936, launching a new era of motor scooter craze in the U.S. It originally used a two-stroke engine and a friction roller drive to the rear wheel until a chain drive was later fitted.

Cushman's Auto-Glide came nipping along at the heels of the Motor Glide just a few months after it went on the market. Prior to the Auto-Glide, Cushman was only an engine manufacturer. Their new scooter launched them into the realm of vehicle makers.

Cushman and Salsbury were fierce competitors throughout the years, but Salsbury left a legacy that is still with us today. In 1938 the Self-Shifting Transmission was released in the Motor Glide Model 50 and Model 60. The Self-Shifting Transmission is essentially what we know today as a Continuously Variable Transmission (CVT). A revolution in its day, the CVT is now standard equipment on the overwhelming majority of new scooters. America's contribution to the development of scooters is largely overshadowed by Italy, and as such, the notable CVT-equipped Salsburys are relatively obscure. During the latter half of the 1930s other scooter companies popped up, but few had the stay-ing power of Salsbury or Cushman.

This 1948 American Salsbury Model 85, owned by John Wiser, is sleek and never went out of style.

(Photo courtesy of Sandra Carr)

Scooters in Italy

After the Second World War, the Italian economy was in shambles. Most manufacturing companies had participated in the war effort and some of them were thereafter banned from making some of the same products after the war that they made during and prior to it. Piaggio was one such example. Their big business had been making military aircraft. With no market or legal ability to do that any longer, they quickly needed a product. The ideal product for Piaggio would use their engineering and manufacturing capabilities while being something that would be useful to the Italian people and well within their reach financially.

> **Scootrivia**
>
> Vespa is the Italian word for wasp. It is an appropriate moniker for a scooter with a curvaceously pointed shape and a buzzing two-stroke engine.

The answer came from designer and engineer Corradino d'Ascanio. The Vespa came with easy-to-change tires, an engine hidden from view, and bodywork to keep wind, water, and road grime off the rider. Shifting was on the grip so that it would be easier for novice riders to use. It addressed most of the shortfalls of contemporary motorcycles in the context of being used as day-to-day transportation. Because Piaggio had invested heavily in equipment to form sheet metal, the Vespa was made of pressed steel. After a few short years, Vespa expanded their operations and several foreign firms were producing Vespas under license in Germany, France, England, and even India.

Other manufacturers had similar ideas about the future of personal transportation in Italy. Innocenti came up with a different kind of scooter concept that reflected their capabilities. A tubing and pipe manufacturer, they used bent steel tubes for their frames. The early Lambretta scooters produced by Innocenti were more like Cushman and Salsbury scooters. Engines hung off tube frames that were not as fully dressed in bodywork as the Vespa.

Other manufacturers in Italy also tried to get in on the scooter craze. Some did and had moderate success; most manufactured a small volume of scooters by comparison to the giants.

This vintage Lambretta looks brand new.

(Photo by Bev Brinson)

Timeline of Notable Scooters

Following is a timeline of notable scooters:

♦ 1936 Salsbury Motor Glide: The first scooter from Salsbury, the Motor Glide launched a scooter craze in America during the depression.

♦ 1936 Cushman Auto-Glide: On the market a few months after Salsbury, Cushman expanded their engine company into scooters.

♦ 1938 Salsbury Motor Glide Model 50: Given what was termed a Self-Shifting Transmission, it was the first scooter with an automatic Continuously Variable Transmission. A revolution in its day, the CVT is now the dominant scooter transmission.

◆ 1946 Piaggio Vespa 98CC: The first production scooter from Vespa. Designed to make two-wheel riding more user friendly.

◆ 1947 Lambretta Model A: A rivalry was born with the Lambretta that played out over the next few decades. Vespa or Lambretta would up the ante, and the other would then raise the stakes again.

◆ 1954 Vespa 150 GS: Vespa's first sport model, the GS sported a fourth gear and 10-inch wheels. It was more expensive and more powerful than previous Vespas and represented scooters moving away from being "no-frills" transportation.

◆ 1957 Lambretta TV175: Adding a fourth gear and 10-inch wheels to the Lambretta line, the Turismo Veloce 175 was aimed squarely at the Vespa GS and a move upmarket. Vespa's retort came in the form of the highly vaunted 160 GS.

◆ 1958 Honda Cub: The little giant of the scooter universe, Honda's Cub has been in production for nearly 50 years. While many things have changed, the overall shape and layout have not. The Cub in all of its forms uses a manual transmission with motorcycle-style controls, medium-size wheels, and a step-through body with a basic leg shield but little additional bodywork. Since 1958 it has sold over 50 million units, which makes it the world's most popular two-wheeler by a landslide.

◆ 1960 Harley Davidson Topper: A major break from tradition for Harley, it had a fiberglass body, making it among the first plastic-bodied scooters.

◆ Sears and Montgomery Ward: Both retailers sold scooters during the 1950s and 1960s. Sears sold Cushmans and Vespas, rebadged under the Allstate name. Montgomery Ward sold Mitsubishi Silver Pigeons and Lambrettas under the Riverside name. Both companies sold sizable quantities of scooters to Americans either in stores or through their catalogs.

◆ Vespa P Series: The culmination of the two-stroke, manual-shift Vespa. The P series has been offered in different guises since 1977, making it the longest-running Vespa model. In the U.S. the current iteration is the PX150.

- 1986 Honda Helix: The current crop of maxi-scooters can trace their roots to the venerable Helix. It has had a 20-year production run with only minimal changes. With a 250cc engine, a laid-back seating position, and a long wheelbase, it's ideal as a scooter for touring and cruising around on.

- 1996 Vespa ET2 and ET4: These two models brought Vespa into the realm of modern, automatic scooters. The four-stroke engine of the ET4 was also something new for Vespa.

Unique Designs Throughout History

Many scooters have been adapted for other uses by both enterprising individuals and manufacturers. Some were complete disasters, but others proved themselves to be quite useful at transporting passengers and large items efficiently.

Wartime Scooters

During WWII the U.S. military dropped a few Cushman scooters from planes along with paratroopers so that they would have ground transportation where they landed. The Airborne models were rarely used, but were an interesting idea. Many other concepts followed from other manufacturers, but few saw action.

Workhorse Scooters

A couple of workhorse scooters should also be mentioned.

Cushman Package Kar

One of the first workhorse scooters, the Package Kar had a pair of wheels in front and one at the rear. It was available with a storage box up front or as a partially bare chassis for customers with more specialized needs. Apparently this approach was considered to be putting the cart before the horse because most three-wheeled, scooter-based work vehicles since then have had one wheel in front and two at the rear.

Kick Start _____

The Vespa Ape was also made under license in other parts of the world. Bajaj currently makes an evolution of it in India in three body styles: pickup truck, cargo van, and autorickshaw. The volume they sell has made them the world's largest producer of three-wheelers.

Vespa Ape–First Three-Wheeled Delivery Vehicle

As with the first Vespa, the Ape took earlier concepts and refined them with clever touches. A rear cargo box allowed larger and bulkier items to be loaded without obstructing the rider's forward view.

The original Ape (Italian for bee) was basically a scooter up front with a truck bed in the back, perched atop a pair of rear wheels. As the Ape evolved, it became more versatile and specialized. A cab around the driver was eventually added for weather protection.

The history of scooters is extremely rich and broad, and this is just a small slice of it. From the beginning the scooter has been the unsung hero of the transportation universe. It's been to war, it's been to work, it's been around the world. The rest of the world takes for granted the contributions of the scooter, but Americans are rediscovering scooters and how versatile they are.

The Least You Need to Know

- The history of scooters spans more than a century.
- America was the first major scooter-producing country.
- Scooters know how to work as hard as they play.
- You'll find scooters in places where inexpensive and efficient transportation is needed.

Chapter 2

How Scooters Work

In This Chapter

- ◆ What makes a scooter a scooter?
- ◆ Engine types and traits
- ◆ Plastic or steel?
- ◆ Brakes

Though scooters look very simple, they are actually more complex than meets the eye. In this chapter we break down the scooter to find out what makes it go, what makes it stop, and what makes it different from its two-wheeled cousin, the motorcycle.

Scooter vs. Motorcycle

In the beginning, there were bicycles, and they were good. Then humankind realized bicycles could be better if an engine were bolted into the frame. And so the first motorcycles were born.

As bicycles with engines, they had more in common with mopeds than the sport bikes and cruisers that dominate motorcycle dealer showrooms these days. From this early beginning, motorcycles evolved to be more specialized. A series of natural selections led to the motor scooter as we know it today, with its step-through frame, diminutive size, and often-small wheels.

To Shift or Not to Shift

For decades, nearly all scooters were manual shift. The 1980s and 1990s saw the rise of the *Continuously Variable Transmission (CVT)* automatic scooter, which now dominates the market. In the United States recently there have been only a few choices for manual-shift scooters. On most manual scooters, the clutch is operated by the left hand, and the left grip twists to shift the gears. This is contrary to contemporary motorcycles, on which the left foot operates the shifter. As with a car, transmission is a personal preference that can be influenced by the intended usage of the vehicle. In a lot of stop-and-go traffic, an automatic can be wonderful. In other situations shifting can be quite fun. Having a manual transmission as one of your buying criteria does limit your choices, but it does give you a more vintage authentic riding experience.

def•i•ni•tion

A **Continuously Variable Transmission (CVT)** commonly has two variable pulleys and a rubber drive belt. Unlike automotive automatic transmissions, a CVT has no gears.

A CVT uses two pulleys, and a rubber belt to offer a range of ratios for the engine to use. Think of a 10-speed bicycle; now think of one with 24 speeds. On both bikes there are multiple gears on the pedal shaft and multiple gears on the rear axle. CVTs work in much the same way as a multi-speed bicycle. They have a minimum gear ratio and maximum gear ratio. However, instead of having several distinct ratios in between, a CVT has an infinite number of possible ratios between the maximum and minimum. Because there are no distinct gears, there is no sensation of shifting up. You rev up the engine, the clutch engages, and the engine climbs to a certain speed and stays there until you let off the throttle or until you hit top speed. For someone who has never piloted any vehicle with a CVT, it can be a very strange experience. Once you get used to it, most conventional automatic transmissions seem clunky and outdated by comparison.

Scooters that are manual usually clutch and shift on the left-hand grip. Simply pull in the clutch and turn, but be sure you release the throttle on the right grip. Otherwise, you may pop a wheelie.

(Photo by Bev Brinson)

You may be wondering how a CVT changes ratio if it does not have any gears. The two pulleys widen and narrow to change their effective diameters. Going back to the bicycle analogy, when you take off from a stop, you use your smallest front sprocket and the largest rear sprocket. The front, or variator, pulley widens to make the belt diameter small up front. The rear pulley is as narrow as possible at this point to provide strong acceleration off the line. At top speed, the variator pulley has narrowed to allow a large belt diameter, while the rear pulley has widened to decrease belt diameter. The effect is like switching to your biggest pedal sprocket and your smallest axle sprocket on your bicycle.

Now that you know *what* the CVT does, the *how* is pretty simple. The variator pulley has cylindrical roller weights behind the inner pulley half. As the engine revs up, these weights are slung outward, which pushes the two halves of the variator pulley closer together to increase the belt diameter. How much a roller weighs determines whether a scooter will be more biased toward strong acceleration or a high top speed. A spring holds the rear pulley halves close together, but as the belt speed increases, it forces the pulley halves farther apart against the pressure of the spring. Simple mechanical control systems mean automatic scooters have a very uncomplicated way of transmitting power from the engine to the rear wheel.

The downside of the simple CVT is that there is always a compromise made between acceleration and top speed. Computer control helps eliminate this by quickly adapting to rider inputs on the throttle. It is more expensive to engineer and produce, and is still rare on scooters.

Scootrivia

Computer-controlled CVTs are prevalent in automobiles that are CVT-equipped. Recently, they have begun to trickle down to two-wheelers. Suzuki's Burgman 650 is the first scooter sold in the U.S. with an electronically controlled CVT. It also has a sport mode that enables the rider to manually shift between six computer-determined "gear" ratios.

Step-Through Design Instead of Leg-Over

A step-through frame is the most obvious difference between scooters and traditional motorcycles. This design feature offers comfort, wind protection, and the preservation of modesty for women wearing skirts. The step-through is not only what defines scooters to most people, but also is what made them so popular.

The Kymco People is a very popular 50cc step-through design scooter.

(Photo courtesy of Kymco)

Throughout the years, the utter practicality of stepping into your bike and sitting on it like a chair or stool has made the scooter a trans-generational machine that could be ridden by young and old alike. Obviously, women in skirts could ride it, but the leg shield would protect the businessman in his suit from puddles and road debris.

Veteran motorcyclists are being won over by the segment of large (400cc and up) touring scooters that are gaining popularity. Many mature riders who found it difficult to saddle up on large touring bikes find big scooters very easy to climb onto. They also tend to appreciate the superb wind protection and comfortable seating positions that are afforded by a step-through body.

Ergonomically, most scooters have an advantage over the two most popular types of motorcycle in America. Unlike sport bikes, the riding position is not hunched over. A rider's back is not arched unnaturally and his or her weight is not being pushed onto the grips, which prevents sore arms and wrists. Though cruiser motorcycles have almost the opposite seating position, many have their own ergonomic drawbacks.

Riders of automatic scooters have also discovered that they can hang several grocery sacks from bag hooks and keep them centered with their feet. With a couple of bungee cords, it's also possible to strap small boxes to the floorboard. Versatility is one of the traits that has endeared step-through bodies, and scooters, to millions of people the world over.

Bodywork and Storage

Major mechanical systems are quite visible on most motorcycles. Those components tend to get hidden away behind bodywork on scooters. The rationale for secluding those items is that bodywork keeps oil, grease, grime, and heat off the rider and passenger. Other bodywork, like the leg shield, helps provide wind protection to the rider. Along with the leg shield, the floorboard offers some splash protection on wet roads or puddles.

Scooters also offer more standard storage than most conventional motorcycles. Newer automatic models typically offer space under the seat, and sometimes in a leg-shield glove compartment. Manual shift and vintage scooters rarely have storage under the seat, but have larger glove boxes, and more choices for optional carrying racks.

It's not at all unheard of for scooter riders to recount making grocery-store runs on the scooter. Bag hooks in the step-through space also make carrying items easier. This is especially true on automatic scooters that have both brakes on the handlebars. A flat floorboard with a good bag hook offers a lot of room for bags of stuff.

If your scooter enables you to put your feet on the passenger pegs, you would be amazed at how much stuff you can lug around. In developing nations people carry livestock, oversized crates, and entire families on their scooters. Scooters are antlike in their ability to carry large amounts of weight; and despite being small, they offer more storage than most motorcycles.

Ample storage can be found under the seat on most scooters. But maxi scooters, such as the Suzuki Burgman, enable you to take it all with you.

(Photo courtesy of Suzuki)

Body composition is a longstanding debate that rages in the scooter community. When scooters first came into existence, steel was the wonder material that nearly everything was made of. Within the last 40 years, plastics have taken over many of the roles that metals once played. Most new scooters now have plastic body panels over a steel frame. A few new scooters still use steel for the bodywork.

There are advantages and drawbacks to both sides. Though steel can be repaired at an automotive body shop, it can be expensive, depending on the damage. Replacing plastic panels usually takes very little time once the part is in, and the costs can be reasonable on some models. Steel is also known to rust, and plastic isn't. In the salty sea air of coastal cities, steel bodywork can rust easily. Though modern steel scooters are usually given special corrosion-preventing primers, they are not effective forever. An accident on a metal scooter can also expose bare metal and create the possibility of rust forming later on. Even with those disadvantages, steel scooters do have a different sound and feel about them. New ones generally have a feeling of solidity that a number of plastic-bodied scooters do not have.

Even though new Vespas use steel for much of their bodywork, many large body panels are actually painted plastic. The PX 150, Stella, and Bajaj may still be mostly metal, but there are a few plastic parts to be found. If you are truly obsessed with all-steel construction, you have to go vintage. Instead of focusing on what material your scooter is made of, you are better off finding the one that suits your needs and does the things you want. If a sport model 50cc scooter is a perfect fit, then no metal-bodied scooter can really compete with the likes of a Kymco Super 9 or Aprilia SR50 Ditech. If zooming down the interstate at 85 mph is on your agenda, then steel is obviously out of the question. A quality scooter that suits your wants and needs will make you happy regardless of which materials make up its composition.

Shiftless Motorcycles Blur the Line

Over the past few years the division between traditional motorcycle and scooter has become less clear. Aprilia often billed the big-wheel Scarabeo 500 as an "automatic motorcycle." CF Moto took the idea even further by putting an automatic scooter engine into a frame that looks like a conventional motorcycle. The CPI GTR has sport-bike looks, 17-inch wheels, and no step-through, but it has a scooter engine, suspension, and a CVT.

The CPI GTR offers a bold, motorcycle leg-over design all with the convenience of a twist-and-go transmission.

(Photo courtesy of CPI-USA)

Several recent motorcycle shows have been peppered with automatic motorcycle concepts. Italjet had a concept known as the Amarcord. Reminiscent of 1920s single-cylinder motorcycles, it is powered by a 150cc scooter engine. Honda has shown a few maxi-scooter concepts with engine displacements above 750cc.

To further muddy the waters, Honda is also releasing a 700cc V-twin motorcycle with an automatic transmission. With the words "twist and go" so strongly identified with modern scooters, it is easy to see why other automatic two-wheelers cloud the issue of what is and is not a scooter. American manufacturer Ridley makes CVT automatic cruisers paired with V-twin engines. Yamaha has released the FJR1300AE, which retains manual shift but dispenses with the manually operated clutch. Automatic transmissions may be most popular with scooters, but automatics are finding new niches among several motorcycle genres.

A new crop of automatic motorcycles will likely cause the definition of scooter to drop automatic transmission as a trait. It will likely revert to describing a smaller motorcycle that has a step-through body, an engine and transmission that also act as a rear swing arm, and that generally has smaller wheels.

Motor + Pedals = Moped

Peruse eBay or do a web search for scooter and many of the results returned often use the word moped in the title. Unless a vehicle has pedals and a motor, it is not a moped. This gets confused because some states have special regulations for mopeds. These regulations are often so broadly written that any two-wheeled vehicle is lumped into a "moped" or "motorized bicycle" category on the basis of top speed or engine size. Check your state and local laws before making a purchase intended for moped classification. Your local DMV can be a great source of information about what can and cannot be registered as a moped.

They will be the ones who process all of your paperwork, and right or wrong, they will have an almost final say on what you can and cannot register. Several state DMVs have links on their websites to the state statutes regulating motorcycles and mopeds.

Scootrivia
Most true mopeds have a hollow frame that does double duty as the fuel tank.

Two-Stroke vs. Four-Stroke

Two-stroke engines were the dominant engine format for scooters because they are simple, inexpensive, and powerful, yet compact. The

Achilles heel of the two-stroke is that they tend to pollute more than four-stroke engines, which are now dominating the new scooter market. Even though four-strokes are more complicated and expensive to produce, they have lower emissions and in modern scooters are making similar power outputs to vintage two-strokes of similar displacement.

What Are Strokes and How Many Do I Need?

A stroke refers to the piston moving up or down in the cylinder. In a two-stroke engine a piston moves down once, and up once, during one combustion cycle for a grand total of two strokes. In a four-stroke, the piston moves down to suck in air and fuel, and then moves up to compress it. The mixture is then ignited and the piston moves down again. Finally it moves up to push all the exhaust gasses out. This adds up to four piston movements, or strokes, per combustion cycle.

The four-stroke engine is more complex because it uses valves to control combustion. An intake valve (or multiple valves) open to let air and fuel get sucked into the engine. After the valve closes, the piston begins to compress the fuel and air mixture. Once fully compressed, the spark plug ignites the fuel and air and it expands, pushing the piston downward. The exhaust valve (also multiple in some cases) opens and the piston pushes the exhaust gas out of the cylinder. The cycle then repeats.

Two-strokes do things quite differently. As the piston moves up in the cylinder, it sucks fuel and air into a part of the engine known as the crankcase. As it moves downward, the air is then pushed through a port into the cylinder. The piston rises again, compressing the fuel and air. The spark plug ignites and the piston moves downward. Some exhaust gas escapes through a port as it expands. The incoming fuel and air pushes out the rest and the cycle repeats itself.

Horsepower or Torque?

Four-stroke scooters tend to have more *torque* than two-strokes. Typically, a two-stroke can make higher *horsepower* numbers than a four-stroke. This comparison really only tends to matter on 50cc scooters. Above that size, there are very few two-strokes available.

def•i•ni•tion

> **Torque** is the amount of raw force the engine can output. Torque is responsible for enabling you to start from a stop and makes a difference in climbing hills.
>
> **Horsepower** is the amount of torque an engine can produce over a given time. Horsepower plays a major role in achieving top speed.

On most 50cc scooters, the four-strokes are much less powerful than comparable two-strokes. Two-strokes also have more potential to make horsepower gains with performance tuning parts. Theoretically this means that if a two-stroke and four-stroke engine of similar power output were racing one another uphill, the four-stroke would be likely to win. Horsepower is great, but a little torque can be your best friend. If torque is your thing, then there is no replacement for displacement. For storming hills, a bigger engine is usually the ticket, whether two- or four-stroke.

Longevity and Maintenance

The maintenance schedules are quite different between these engine types. A four-stroke requires oil changes at specified intervals, just like a car does. Two-stroke engines burn oil along with fuel, and in order to keep your engine lubricated, you have to make sure it has oil to consume. Four-strokes will also need to have their valves adjusted periodically. When properly maintained, four-stroke engines generally have a longer life before needing major repairs than a similarly maintained two-stroke.

Two-stroke engines may not require regular oil changes or valve adjustments, but they have other needs. Typically spark plug replacements come at shorter intervals than with four-strokes. If a two-stroke engine is not run at wide-open throttle periodically, it can develop nasty carbon deposits on the piston, head, and in the exhaust port. These deposits can hinder performance and fuel economy. Ultimately, a two-stroke engine is likely to need a cylinder and piston rebuild long before a four-stroke engine will need anything similar.

Air or Liquid Cooling?

Air cooling is the prevailing method for regulating engine temperature on scooters. Usually a fan is employed to force air over metal fins to conduct excess heat away from the engine. This process is simple, reliable, and effective in most circumstances. However, as manufacturers attempt to meet new performance and emissions goals they are beginning to adopt liquid cooling systems much like those found in modern cars.

Liquid cooling involves pumping a coolant through the engine and then through a radiator. The benefits typically include a more stable operating temperature and more power, while retaining or lowering the emissions of a similar air-cooled engine. On scooters above 200cc, liquid cooling systems are pretty much standard fare.

So you're asking, "If liquid cooling is so great, why not use it on all scooters?" There are trade-offs in cost, complexity, and maintenance. Liquid-cooled scooters are more expensive to produce, and consequently have higher retail prices. They also require cooling-system maintenance just like a car. The system needs to be flushed periodically and refilled with water and antifreeze. Though many owners will not directly notice this, a liquid cooling system does make working on a scooter a bit more difficult.

For many, the benefits outweigh the drawbacks. Sport scooter enthusiasts generally prefer liquid cooling for tuning purposes, particularly when it comes to two-strokes. Modifying a scooter to make significantly more power tends to mean it will give off more heat than a stock engine. Liquid cooling helps prevent temperature spikes and seizing on tuned engines.

Scootrivia

Over several decades and iterations, Honda has sold over 50 million Cub style bikes. Not easily pigeonholed, the original Cub and its descendants combine some of the features of scooters, mopeds, and conventional motorcycles. Honda's sales alone make the Cub the most popular style of motorized two-wheeler on the planet. Several other manufacturers have copied the formula and have added to the number of Cub-style bikes traversing the world's roads.

CVT, Clutchless, or "Automatic"?

While the CVT may be the most common automatic transmission on scooters, it is not the only one to have ever been used. Clutchless manual-shift transmissions have been available, most notably on the Honda C70 Passport of the late 1970s and early 1980s. Shifting the gears is not the most difficult part of riding a manual-shift scooter. Using the clutch is what usually requires the most practice and attention. Honda kept the manual-shift layout of the conventional motorcycle on the later iterations of the Cub, but it replaced the manual clutch with an automatic clutch. Control layout is almost like a conventional motorcycle, with the notable absence of a clutch lever on the left-hand grip.

In the world of Chinese scooters, there are also some being made with single-speed chain-drive systems. These are typically found on the lowest-quality scooters coming out of China and are often sold by dishonest sellers who generally advertise them as "automatic." As you will see throughout this book, we recommend buying your scooter from a reputable and preferably local dealer to avoid this type of pitfall.

Riding a chain-driven scooter is like putting a manual transmission car into third gear at all times. On level ground it will pull away from a stop slowly, but will eventually get up to speed. When it reaches the top of the gear, the engine will buzz away and you will be at your top speed.

Those who have ever made the mistake of slotting the shifter into third instead of first at a stoplight can readily imagine how sluggish chain-driven scooters are. Those who have accidentally tried taking off up a hill in third gear can also share in a hearty laugh over the futility of even attempting it. Futile is a most accurate way to describe trying to climb a hill on a scooter with a chain-drive transmission. Even with significant momentum the engine will usually not have sufficient torque to get up the hill quickly, and the completely inappropriate gearing only worsens things. Most chain-driven scooters will not climb hills at all if not already running at full speed prior to attempting ascent.

Without the ability to even get out of its own way, this type of scooter is unsafe on that basis alone. With poor quality, dodgy brakes, and minimal suspension, most of these scooters can fairly and accurately be called junk and are unfit for use by anyone.

> **Oil Slick** _____
> Single-speed chain drives are the equivalent of a child's bicycle, while a CVT would be comparable to an 18-speed bicycle. Where the CVT offers a wide range of gear ratios, the single speed only offers one. These systems are commonly found on the cheapest Chinese 50cc scooters, and should be avoided at all costs.

The Breakdown on Brakes

Though the stuff that makes a scooter go is important, the brakes are arguably even more important. There are many times when you will need to stop, sometimes very quickly.

Brakes work by converting kinetic energy into heat by increasing friction on the rolling assembly of the wheel and tire. One of the primary goals of a brake engineer is to find a way to very quickly turn friction into heat and to then dissipate the heat quickly enough that the brakes will be operable for long periods of time.

Disc Brakes

Ever grabbed something that was spinning to stop it? That's the basic principle of how a disc brake works. A metal rotor or disc spins with your wheel and a caliper clamps down on it when the brake lever is pulled. The friction between the pads and the rotor slows down and stops the wheel.

As mentioned, this can create serious amounts of heat. Disc brakes have superior cooling traits that make them more consistent than drum brakes, particularly after hard use. Because a disc brake can shed excess heat very quickly, it is unlikely to overheat the friction materials. Rotors are also less likely to become warped, unless the brake system is abused or put through punishing conditions like those seen on a race track. As friction compounds overheat, their ability to convert motion energy into heat is severely diminished. In practical terms, excessively hot brakes increase the distance it takes to stop. Warped brakes also do not work as effectively because they prevent the caliper from uniformly clamping the rotor, which also increases braking distances.

Modern scooters overwhelmingly have at least a front disc brake, but there are a few holdouts with front drum brakes. Several higher-performance scooters have disc brakes on the rear wheel as well.

Drum Brakes

Drum brakes theoretically offer more initial bite than disc brakes. Though they have more initial bite, as heat builds up in a brake drum it becomes less effective. The heat-retention properties of drum brakes make them somewhat more prone to warping or going out of round than disc brakes. Cable-operated drum brakes are typically less expensive to engineer and manufacture than hydraulic discs, which is why they are still commonly used for rear brakes on most scooters under 200cc. Weight transfers forward when braking. Conventional wisdom says that around 70 percent of the braking on a two-wheeler is done by the front wheel. With so much of the braking done up front, a rear disc would be overkill on many scooters. Cable actuation is the norm for drum brakes on scooters. Cables are simple and reliable, but they do require periodic adjustment as they stretch a bit over time.

Anti-lock Brake Systems (ABS)

Anti-lock brake systems have become standard safety features on many new cars, but they are not very common on two-wheeled vehicles. As on cars, ABS promises shorter braking times and safer braking. It should prevent lockup in most situations, which should keep the vehicle upright and stable. Automotive ABS systems are intended to prevent lockup so a driver can still turn and maneuver while braking. Braking during a turn will still destabilize a scooter or motorcycle. Attempting to corner and brake hard will have consequences even if the wheels do not lock up. The point of anti-lock brakes on motorcycles is more to prevent the straight-line skidding that happens due to wheel lockup. When a tire skids, the delicate balance of a two-wheeler is upset and there is a risk of crashing. If the system prevents a skid, the bike is more likely to stay upright.

ABS brake systems work by constantly monitoring the speed of each wheel. When the ABS computer detects braking and sees that the two wheels are moving at vastly different speeds, it decides that one or both wheels have locked up. The computer then pulses the brakes to correct the condition. Some systems also add gyro sensors to detect g-forces in addition to wheel speed. If both wheels lock up, the computer can determine that the vehicle is completely stopped, and, as such, it may not pulse the brakes. A gyro sensor helps the computer determine whether or not the two-wheeler is actually stopped with both wheels not moving. If the sensors do not all concur, then the anti-lock system should spring into action. The likelihood of both front and rear brakes locking up simultaneously is fairly low, but obviously some companies see it as enough of a possibility to take another step to prevent brake lockup.

Such an intricate system means that anti-lock brakes are typically an expensive option on top-tier scooters. Be wary of bargain-priced scooters, particularly from China, claiming to have ABS. What they have is a system that limits the effectiveness of your brakes. They do not have the electronic hardware and software to sense lockup. So you get less brake power than you would need on smooth, dry pavement, and less than what you need on uneven or wet surfaces. These so-called anti-lock systems also are only built to operate on the front brake, which means that if the rear brake is applied too hard and too quickly, there is nothing to stop the rear wheel from locking up and skidding. One of the biggest reasons for the existence of ABS on motorcycles is the ability to prevent lockup at both ends of the bike.

> **Kick Start**
>
> A true anti-lock brake system has several sensors and an electronic brain to recognize and stop wheel lockup. These are usually only found on high-end, flagship-model scooters

Linked Systems

Instead of having the front and rear brakes completely separate, linked brake systems let the rear lever control the rear and some of the front brake. The front lever offers additional braking on the front wheel as needed.

Linked braking was designed to help less-experienced riders stop faster and more safely. Motorcyclists learned over the years that a combination of front and rear braking was more effective than either alone.

It also took a lot of experience to figure out the proper proportion to use. Linked braking takes away some of the guesswork and tends to decelerate a vehicle more quickly and with less chance of locking up the wheels.

Linked systems typically are proportioned so the rear brake does 50–70 percent of the braking and the front does 30–50 percent. Many very experienced riders dislike them because it is a very different experience from a traditional brake setup. Linked brake systems are almost exclusively found on motorcycles and scooters with disc brakes front and rear. Usually this kind of braking system is found on bigger scooters. It is also commonly used in conjunction with real anti-lock braking systems.

The Least You Need to Know

+ A step-through is the most common scooter trait.
+ If it's a 50cc, a two-stroke is preferable.
+ Shifting narrows down your choices a bit.
+ Automatic does not necessarily mean CVT.
+ Good brakes are the key to safety.

Chapter 3

Scooter Matchmaking

In This Chapter

- ◆ Picking the right new, used, or vintage scooter
- ◆ Other expenses to budget for
- ◆ Buyer beware, street legality, and warranty issues
- ◆ What to look for in a dealer

Finding the perfect scooter is a bit like finding the perfect man or woman. There is no one perfect scooter for everyone, but there may be one out there that is right for you. Just as with that special someone, the wisdom of Motown and your mama apply to scooters: "You better shop around."

You read that and either chuckled or groaned, but you're still thinking, "That's all well and good, but where do I actually start?" If you honestly answer the questions in this chapter, the best scooter for you will become apparent. The first step is to get your priorities figured out. Let's kick things off by determining how much engine you will need.

Do I Ever Want to Ride on the Interstate?

In some states, there are minimum-displacement or power-output requirements for riding on interstates or controlled-access highways. In others, it is more a matter of being able to keep up with traffic. Regardless of local requirements, you will want a scooter that has a *cruising speed* that matches up with the speeds you plan to ride. When looking at a model, you will often hear about *top speed*. If the top speed you are quoted is the speed you need to go most of the time, you will want to consider a more powerful scooter. You need to have power and speed in reserve for passing, ascending hills, and riding into headwinds.

Braking, handling, and stability are additional concerns to those who want to ride on fast highways. A good freeway bike will be stable enough to maintain a lane even when subjected to gusts and crosswinds. Essentially this means that a good highway-capable scooter will have some bulk to it. It also shouldn't present too much of a profile to be caught by the wind. Beyond aerodynamics and weight, the wheels, tires, and suspension should be of concern. Being able to maintain speed and make quick maneuvers when necessary can make all the difference between a near miss and a serious accident.

def•i•ni•tion

The **cruising speed** is a speed where you still have power for accelerating, passing, or climbing hills.

The **top speed** is the fastest your scooter will go in normal conditions

A tire-tread pattern that won't vibrate on grooved pavement is really important at high speeds. Disconcerting is one word to describe your handlebars shaking in your hands, though there are many expletives that probably do better justice to that eerie sensation.

Tire grip and speed rating also make a difference. If you really want to ride on the freeway, you want tires with a higher speed rating. A speed rating not only tells you the maximum speed, but it gives you an idea about the grip of the rubber compounds and tread pattern being used. Higher means that you can ride faster in a straight line and that you'll have more capability around turns. Higher speed ratings also shorten the distance needed for braking. Properly balanced wheels may not matter all that much around town, but as wheel speeds increase, imbalances also can cause vibrations. Some of which may make the ride and handling less predictable, and certainly will make things less pleasant.

The overall suspension geometry also makes a difference. Wheelbase, wheel travel (up and down movement), and many other things make some scooters very suited for higher-speed use. A longer wheelbase tends to increase stability at high speeds. On the other hand, it usually decreases agility, particularly at low speeds.

Finally, braking should be on your list of attributes to look for when judging highway capability. You need to be able to stop quickly and smoothly. Progressive bite is desirable, as grabby brakes can lead to lockup in panic situations. High speeds mean you need to be able to stop quickly.

What Local Factors Should I Consider?

As any good real estate agent will tell you, it's all about location, location, location. Scootering is the same way. In a warm, sunny paradise you might be able to ride year around happily on almost any scooter. If you live in any other part of the country where such a climate seems mythical, many local factors will come into play.

When the Wind Comes Sweeping Down the Plains

High winds can greatly reduce your speed when riding against them. They can also really toss some vehicles around. Lightweight scooters with a lot of surface area tend to be the most affected. It can be a very troubling experience for new and experienced riders alike, and is especially apparent above 60 mph.

Strong headwinds also can fatigue a rider. When test-riding a scooter you want to use for highway riding, it's important to find out how it performs in the wind. It will make a huge difference in your comfort, stability, and miles per gallon.

Altitude Affects Your Scooter's Attitude

Elevation directly affects the performance of an engine. Your scooter will generate less power in an environment where the air is less dense. When the air is less dense the engine cannot burn as much fuel and it will not make the same amount of power. This is part of why getting a test ride is important. A scooter that might be fast along coastal roads

Oil Slick

Hills will negatively affect your speed. If you live in a hilly area, you should consider a more powerful engine. There is no replacement for displacement.

around Miami just above sea level will definitely have somewhat dulled acceleration and a lower top speed in a place like Denver. The hill-climbing ability of a scooter at high altitude will also be diminished.

Not Just a Fair-Weather Friend

Scooters have leg shields to protect the rider from inclement weather. Some scooters also come with windscreens or provisions for them. The size and shape of those items determine how much airflow they deflect. In a cold or rainy climate, more protection is better. In a hot climate, more airflow keeps you cooler. A test ride will quickly make it clear how much weather protection a scooter offers.

A Quick and Dirty Guide to Size vs. Speed

The chart below gives some broad guidelines about what can generally be expected from unmodified scooters in the following engine size ranges.

Displacement	Cruising Speed	Top Speed
50cc	20-30mph	30-50mph
80cc	35mph	45mph
125-150cc	45mph	55-70mph
200-250cc	60-65mph	70-80mph
400+cc	70-80mph	90-120mph

There is a very large range in speed in the 50cc class because some are two-stroke and others are four-stroke. Those differences will be discussed in more detail later. 50cc scooters are also typically sold with restrictor devices to govern the top speed to 30 mph. Removing them increases top speed and cruising speed. It usually also helps acceleration. In the 125-to-150cc class there is also a broad range of cruising and top speeds due to size, weight, aerodynamics, and power output of the engine.

How Often Do I Plan to Carry a Passenger?

If your response is anything other than, "I don't plan to ever have passengers," then you need to follow it up with, "How much do my typical passenger and I weigh together?" You need to find out what the maximum load weight of the vehicle is in order to determine if it will meet your needs. If you and your usual passenger weigh 300 lbs, and the scooter has a maximum load capacity of 250 lbs, you will not be safe or comfortable. The load capacity is the difference between the *gross weight* and the *curb weight* (not to be confused with *dry weight*). If a scooter has a gross weight of 500 lbs and a curb weight of 240 lbs, it means the scooter isn't capable of carrying more than 260 lbs of people and cargo. Some scooters only have enough seating for one rider, and it is inadvisable to ride with a passenger.

As with hills, passengers will affect your acceleration and cruising speed. However, unlike hills, passengers and cargo affect braking and handling. With a passenger aboard, it will take longer to come to a stop and you will find that turning requires more effort and skill.

def•i•ni•tion

Dry weight is common in brochures and other sales literature about how much a scooter or motorcycle weighs. It is the weight of the scooter alone, and as the name implies, without fluids like fuel, coolant, lubricants, etc.

Unlike dry weight, **curb weight** refers to a vehicle full of necessary fluids and as you might find it sitting by the curb in ready-to-ride condition.

Gross weight is an upper maximum weight for the vehicle, its fluids, occupants, and cargo. Going above this weight is unsafe

So Can I Just Buy the Red One?

Color may be the first thing you notice about a scooter, but it should be the last factor influencing your decision. Bright colors offer better visibility, but color choice is a personal decision to be made only after picking out the right model for your needs.

Try It on for Size

Buying a scooter is a lot like buying a jacket. Fit is everything. All of us have walked into a store and found a jacket that looks perfect. It has the style, the features, and everything you feel like you could ever want from a jacket. Even better, it's on sale. But wouldn't you know it, when you go to try one on, it fits well in the shoulders, but the sleeves are too short. Or it's too tight around your stomach.

Unlike cars, scooters do not offer much in terms of ergonomic adjustability. If you pick the wrong one, you will be at best uncomfortable, and at worst unsafe. Your personal concept of scary gets seriously redefined when your handlebar and knees are trying to occupy the same space in the middle of a tight turn.

Like a Glove

A scooter that feels tailor-made for your unique build is a beautiful thing. Your feet will fit perfectly on the floorboard while clad in the riding boots or shoes you will normally wear. Ideally, you will have both feet flat on the pavement with the scoot (an abbreviated slang term for scooter) off the center stand. At a bare minimum, you need to be able to put the balls of both feet on the ground. If you can't do that, find a lower scooter. Real roads aren't as smooth, level, or free of debris as a showroom floor. Suddenly being on your tiptoes seems like a bad idea.

Sitting Pretty

Not all scooters have the same seating position. On some of them you will sit very upright, while on others you will sit more reclined with your feet forward. It all comes down to personal preference. The different sizes and styles will also have different floorboard positions and foot space on them.

Bring a Friend

If you plan to routinely carry a passenger, then bring someone the size and weight of your usual passenger. It will quickly narrow down which scooters are really built for two.

Go Around the Block a Few Times

Different scooters ride, handle, and perform differently, and riding them is the only way to find out which one will make you happiest. One with 10-inch wheels and one with 16-inch wheels will ride and handle very differently. Wheel diameter has a major influence on the suspension geometry. Brakes are another area where you really just have to ride the scooter to see how it compares to others. Some brakes offer a lot of feedback, while others don't. Some bite hard very early, and others are much more gradual.

I Can't Get a Test Ride!

If you are unable to go for a test ride, find as many thorough reviews as you can on the scooters you're interested in. Though not a true replacement for first-hand experience with a machine, it will at least give you an idea of what to expect.

 Kick Start

Be prepared. Be licensed. No car dealer will let an unlicensed customer take a test drive. Scooter dealers require motorcycle licenses for test rides. If you want a test ride, take the MSF course and get licensed before going shopping.

What Should I Budget for Buying a Scooter?

The initial purchase of a scooter involves costs beyond just the bike itself. The price at your dealer may be different than what you see on a manufacturer's website because of variables like freight, prep, local taxes, and fees.

Manufacturer's Suggested Retail Price

The MSRP is just that, a suggestion. As with buying a new car, you will find that there are other costs involved.

Freight

Shipping is another common cost above MSRP. Many dealers simply pass that cost right along without markup, though some do charge above their cost for the freight fee.

Prep

All scooters arrive at the dealer in crates. Many of them do not have the front wheel bolted in. Due to federal laws, the batteries are not installed and the fuel tanks are dry. Lubricants and other fluids are occasionally the responsibility of the dealer. There are also safety checks the dealer is required to perform. All scooters require some amount of prep work, which usually takes 1 to 3 hours. Some dealers charge their shop labor rate for it, while others have a flat fee.

Tax, Title, and License Not Included

Sales tax and documentation fees are also part of the process, but they vary by state and locality.

Out the Door

When shopping you should always ask for the "out the door" or "on the road" price, and be sure to specify whether or not that includes sales tax. This will help you compare apples to apples throughout the buying process. Again, reputable dealers will nearly always give a breakdown of the final price. Often it will be on the price tag.

Budgeting Beyond the Bike Itself

The most common mistake among scooter buyers is budgeting for only the scooter itself. Here we cover some of the associated costs to consider when creating a budget.

Insurance

Insurance varies widely by company and engine displacement. Get quotes before making a final purchase.

Registration and License Plates

Any title fees you paid at the dealer don't cover your real plates when the temporary tags expire.

Consumables

Tires and brake pads don't last as long as their automobile counterparts. Good two-stroke oil is another item to budget into your fuel costs.

Maintenance

Service intervals on scooters come more frequently than they do on cars. Drive belts and roller weights typically need to be replaced between 4,000 and 8,000 miles, depending on model. Oil changes happen between 1,500 and 3,000 miles as scheduled in your owner's manual. Batteries need to be kept charged by riding or with a battery tender. If they aren't, they become an expensive addition to the list of consumables. Manual shift models also require periodic adjustment to the cables.

While these items don't need to be part of your initial purchase budget, maintenance will need to occur down the line and it's an expense to expect.

Helmet

Not required in many states, it's still a must-have for the safety-conscious scooter rider. A good helmet will protect you so that if the unexpected happens you will be more likely to live to ride another day. When developing a budget for a scooter, a helmet should be near the top of your list of associated expenses.

Protective Gear

It's easy to look at jackets, gloves, boots, and riding pants as expensive and unnecessary items, but they are cheaper than a visit to the ER. As with a helmet, good protective gear is a must-have for the rider who cares about safety.

Accessorizing

Windscreens, luggage racks, crash bars, top cases, and chrome accents are common upgrades done at the time of purchase. While these can be added later, some of them make life easier when installed right up front.

How Do I Know if a Scooter Is Street Legal?

A number of scooter sellers claim that their products are street legal. Retailers selling scooters online, and even some brick-and-mortar dealers, are guilty of selling products that are not compliant with the EPA or DOT. Many of these retailers distribute products that are not approved by their states.

Though a few states have been known for being lax about registering almost anything, most are putting more scrutiny on scooters. As local authorities become savvier about what is and is not a legitimately street-legal scooter, more and more buyers find that their applications for vehicle registration are being denied.

Charlatans and Rogues

With the rise in gas prices and the popularity of scooters, there has been an influx of scooters, primarily from China, that are not street legal. To keep costs low and profits high, some importers bring in scooters that do not comply with U.S. emissions and safety standards. Some owners have had luck registering them in states that are lax with the registration process. Other buyers have ended up with very expensive paperweights.

U.S. Department of Transportation

The U.S. DOT has some basic standards that apply to the category of motorcycles, which scooters fall under. Federal law requires side reflectors near both wheels, lights that cannot be turned off, and a *kill switch*. These are very easy things to spot, and any scooter without them is not U.S. DOT compliant. It is also not likely to be EPA certified, either. Without DOT approval it will be almost impossible to register your new scooter.

def•i•ni•tion

Mounted next to the throttle for accessibility, a **kill switch** shuts down the engine. The U.S. Department of Transportation mandates this safety feature on all motorcycles and scooters sold in the American market.

Environmental Protection Agency

The EPA sets emissions standards that vehicles have to comply with. As with DOT standards, scooters are lumped in with motorcycles. The EPA requires manufacturers and importers to go through a certification process to ensure that vehicles meet their emissions requirements. They keep an annual database of manufacturers and models that are certified. Without EPA certification, you are unlikely to be able to get your scooter registered and titled.

No Need to Freak Out

It is very easy to worry about whether or not your scooter will be something you can register and actually ride. Spend some time on the Scooter BBS and you're likely to even hear a sad and horrible story or two from people who bought scooters that were not EPA certified or DOT compliant who later could not get them registered and were unable to hear back from the drop shipper they purchased from. However, the major manufacturers make sure their products comply with DOT regulations and are EPA certified. If you walk into any local retailer for a major brand, you can buy without losing sleep.

Oil Slick

If you live in California, you will also need CARB (California Air Resource Board) certification to be able to register a motor vehicle. CARB certification is similar to EPA certification, but not all EPA certified scooters are CARB approved. You can buy with confidence from a local dealer that sells major brands. Otherwise, consult with CARB before buying anything you are unsure of.

What Should I Look for in a Warranty?

The major brands all offer at least a 1-year limited warranty on parts and labor, and some offer 2 years. These warranties typically cover manufacturing defects on nonconsumable parts like tires, drive belts, roller weights, etc. Some of the smaller importers offer parts-only warranties or a certain period of parts and labor followed by parts only. Some of these companies also limit the warranty to only certain components of the scooter.

The Federal Trade Commission's website has an excellent guide to understanding federal warranty law, and can be found at www.ftc. gov/bcp/conline/pubs/buspubs/warranty.htm. The office of your state's Attorney General can also be helpful in determining the validity of a warranty.

Parts-only warranties should be avoided. The same goes for warranties under a year. Though many Internet sellers claim to offer decent warranties, they often have stipulations that erode the usefulness of said warranty. For example, some sellers require defective parts to be sent in before they send you a replacement. Some will also want to look for the defect and attempt to make sure you didn't cause it before sending you a part for free. Of course, you have to pay for the labor to diagnose and repair the scooter. Other sellers require you to have a licensed, professional scooter mechanic do the initial set-up and prep work. Many scooter shops presently do not work on brands they do not sell or scooters purchased from Internet sellers. Often you do not end up with a meaningful warranty.

Finding a Dealer

A good dealer really makes a difference in your overall ownership experience. A good group to help you find one is the National Motor Scooter Dealer's Association. This organization certifies scooter dealerships that meet specific criteria and agree to a code of conduct. The association also partners with groups of individuals, shops, and manufacturers to promote scooter-friendly policy at local levels of government.

Most states also require dealers or motor vehicles to be registered and licensed. In order to get a license, they have to fulfill several requirements, including having insurance policies.

The best scooter dealers are focused on long-term relationships with their customers. Sure, they want you to buy a scooter, but they want you to come back for your maintenance needs. They want you to come back for your safety gear. A great dealer wants you to come back if you catch the performance tuning bug. Great dealers want to set your friends and family up with scooters as you convert them to scootering with your enthusiasm.

Look for a dealer who treats you with respect. One who understands what you're looking for in a scooter and is ready and able to help you find it. A good service department is another thing to look for. Seek out shops that support your local scooter community. They plan to be in it for the long haul and will be there when you need them. You can buy the most stylish and exquisitely engineered scooter with the world's best warranty, but if your dealer is not there for you, your ownership experience will simply not be as pleasant. If the vibe you get from the dealer is not a good one, continue to shop around and find a dealer who makes you happy. Cultivating a positive relationship is something that really benefits both the dealer and the customer.

Buying Used

Buying used is a similar process to buying new. You still need to figure out which scooters will work for you.

As with buying a used car, it is advisable to look for a service history, and possibly also have a mechanical inspection performed prior to making a purchase. For your own safety, it is vital to look for signs of accident damage. Poorly done repairs, or damage that goes without repair, can negatively impact the integrity and handling of a scooter. If there appears to be damage, an inspection goes from being peace of mind to a much higher priority.

There are a number of good deals on used scooters, if you are willing to wait for the right one and if you have money on hand to move quickly. Many scooters have been sold in near-mint condition with very little mileage because the original owner decided that scootering was not what he or she thought it would be. Some just find that they don't ride enough to justify owning it, while others get frightened and simply will not ride anymore.

Buying Vintage

Buying a vintage scooter is a very different process than buying a new or late-model used scooter.

The first step is to get connected with a vintage-oriented scooter shop or club in your area. Some of them are a bit wary of newbies, but they are a very valuable network for finding vintage scooters that come up for sale locally and regionally. If you find your heart set on a Vespa Rally 200 or a Lambretta TV 175, just get the word out and you will get help finding exactly what you are looking for.

A vintage-focused shop or scooter club will also be your best resource for keeping your scoot running in top form, or teaching you how to do it yourself. The newest vintage scooters in the U.S. are still over 20 years old. As such they will need repair, maintenance, and upgrades. In a scooter club you will usually find a number of people who have dealt with almost any mechanical problem you might face. You might also make a few friends in the process.

As with buying new, buying locally is usually the most hassle-free way to go. A major advantage to buying locally is that local scooterists generally know the history of most of the bikes in the area. They can steer you toward or away from certain scoots. When buying from a seller in another location, you have to rely heavily on the seller's word that the scooter truly is as advertised. If you are fortunate to have scooter-savvy friends near the seller, you can have one of them look it over for you, but it's not an ideal substitute for seeing and riding a scooter yourself.

Poorly restored scooters are another issue to beware of. Many companies import and sell restored vintage scooters that are very poorly done. Most of these come from Vietnam and can be found in Internet ads across the country. There are horror stories of these scooters having frames that were bent and broken being haphazardly welded back together. Other tales are of rust being covered by body filler and painted over. Mechanically speaking, engine gaskets are often made of cut-up beer cans. Many parts are hybridized that do not belong together. Scooters that originally came with 8-inch wheels from the factory have been improperly converted to 10-inch wheels. The worst of these scooters are unsafe to ride. Other bad restorations just cost a lot of money to set right.

Several warning signs make spotting such a scooter fairly easy. Two-tone paint was never common from the factory, but has become quite common from fly-by-night restorers. Two-tone in strange color combinations (cream and lime green, for example) is even more obvious. Two-tone paints have been used on custom scooters for years, so it's not a definitive indicator on its own.

Split-saddle seats are another feature that imported restorations have, and two-tone fabric is a pretty good bet that it was not restored stateside.

Excess amounts of chrome also point to this type of bike. The brake and clutch levers were originally aluminum, as were most other bright work parts of the scooters. Chrome is a staple of the custom scene, but many parts on American and European restored scooters don't get plated.

Finally, most of these sellers won't give you a location in their ad, but will offer to ship anywhere for a reasonable fee. They may also make mention of having a few other scooters to sell.

Don't take these as hard and fast rules, but merely guidelines for trying to spot bad restorations.

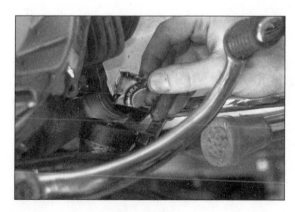

While this scooter is beautiful on the outside, the inside was restored with homemade parts, like this beer can. The owner purchased it online based on nice photos of a decent paintjob. A costly mistake.

(Photo by Bev Brinson)

If you do want to buy a properly restored vintage scooter, ask who did the restoration work and check the receipts. Check with people in the know about whether the details are properly executed if you are interested in buying only a scooter that is restored as accurately as possible.

The Least You Need to Know

- ◆ Scooters are not one-size-fits-all.
- ◆ Buy the scooter that fits your riding needs.
- ◆ Make sure your budget is complete.
- ◆ Avoid headaches: buy from a reputable dealer.
- ◆ Kill the deal if there is no kill switch.

Part 2

What to Expect

There is nothing like the first ride—the purr of the engine, the new found freedom as you pull away. It's an amazing experience and not one to be taken lightly. Learn how to ride safely and how to care for your scooter, and you'll be logging more miles than you ever expected.

We'll also discuss ways to customize your ride inside and out. From custom paint to colored tires, there are options available to express your personality. Flames, flowers, stripes, polka dots—the only limitation is your imagination.

How to Ride

In This Chapter

- ◆ Keeping it legal
- ◆ Helmets: to wear, or not to wear?
- ◆ Riding safely
- ◆ Inclement weather and adverse conditions

We strongly recommend taking a rider-safety course. You'll learn to ride safely and confidently. If that isn't enough, in most states your certificate gets you a motorcycle license. It will also get you discounts on your insurance. The supervised practice will really make a lot of difference in how you ride.

Obeying the Law

Getting pulled over is one of the worst things. Those flashing lights in the rearview mirror, the piercing wail of the sirens. Feeling dread and nervousness in the pit of your stomach. And that's just in a car. Imagine getting pulled over on a scooter. It's not much fun. Everything you have to deal with in a car, but while feeling quite exposed.

The best way to avoid this is to know local traffic and motorcycle regulations and obey them. With a great number of traffic laws being safety oriented, you should follow them for your own safety, if not to avoid being a roadside spectacle.

Rules of the Road Do Apply

You have to obey the same laws on a scooter that you would in a car or on a motorcycle. Riding on sidewalks is, with few exceptions, a no-no. Lane sharing or splitting is also illegal in most places. Passing on the right is also known to get riders into trouble. On any motorized vehicle, you should obey any and all laws that apply to motorized vehicles.

Scooters must obey the same laws as automobiles.

Laws regarding speed limits, stop signs, and everything else also apply, even if the scooter you are on is classified as a moped or motorized bicycle. Legally bicycles have to follow traffic regulations, and even on a motorized bicycle you would have the same legal obligations.

Even if your scooter is considered a moped, you will be safer if you act like you are riding a motorcycle instead of a bicycle. A perfect example is occupying a lane. Some scooter riders meander along the right-hand side of the road where a bicyclist would. The danger in doing this is that drivers of cars, trucks, and SUVs will try to overtake you within the lane. Not only is this illegal on the part of the driver, it is also dangerous to the rider. Generally the automobile drivers who do this are trying to stay as much inside the lane as they possibly can, which means they will more than likely push you more and more toward the curb, if not completely off the road. The area toward the gutter also tends to be packed with the most hazards. Debris, drain grates, potholes, and broken pavement are commonly encountered to the right edge of the road. On roads without curbs, the asphalt often breaks up unexpectedly at the outer edge of the road.

All of these obstacles have the potential to upset your scooter and send you flying. Even on a slow scooter, it's important to ride like you're a motorcycle. Unless riding in a group, you should typically occupy the middle of the lane. This makes you more visible to cars behind you. It also sends a clear signal to those wishing to pass you that they need to do so legally and properly. If or when someone does choose to pass you, maintain your position. Moving over to the right encourages drivers to get too close to you. If a driver will not go completely around, move over, but do so as your last resort.

Most states have laws stating that only one vehicle can occupy a lane at a time. This means riding between cars on the white dashed lines, known as lane splitting or lane sharing, is rarely ever permitted.

Some states do allow for motorcycles to move between stopped traffic to get to the front of the line at a stoplight. The caveat is that the motorcycle has to pull out ahead of the cars and then pick a lane to actually ride in. As mentioned, this varies by state. Check your state's statutes before attempting such a maneuver.

While filtering through stopped traffic may be legit in some places, passing on the right is almost universally illegal. As tempting as it may be to bypass a dozen cars to get up to the stoplight to make a right turn on red, it's best not to do it. Aside from legality issues, *cagers* often have trouble seeing things in their blind spots. If traffic is moving up one car at a time, it would not be unimaginable that a distracted driver might cut in front of you or veer toward the edge of the road.

def•i•ni•tion

Cager is a motorcycle and scooter slang term for those driving cars, in reference to the bodywork that surrounds them like a cage. Though usually it's tongue-in-cheek, it can be a mildly derogatory term.

Some cagers also are downright hostile to those riding on two wheels. When they get passed by smaller and more agile vehicles, rude drivers have been known to block motorcycles and scooters, or to even attempt to run into them or open their car doors at riders. Misery loves company, and there are many miserable souls out on the roads at any given time. Follow the rules of the road both to avoid running afoul of the law as well as for safety's sake.

> **Scootrivia**
>
> California is the only state that allows lane splitting, and law enforcement officers have broad discretion on whether or not it is reckless riding in any given situation.

Do I Need My Motorcycle Endorsement?

Your state's laws will determine whether you need to have a motorcycle license to ride your scooter. Typically you will need one for anything over 50cc, and in several states you need to have one for those as well.

Even if you aren't required to have a motorcycle license to ride your scooter, you owe it to yourself to get proper rider training. If the course you take automatically grants you a license, there is no harm in having the additional endorsement. Even if the safety course you take does not automatically grant you a license, if you can take your exams and become licensed it is generally a fairly easy process in most states. When or if at some point you decide you want a more powerful scooter, or just a second one, having a motorcycle endorsement on your license greatly broadens your horizons when it comes to getting a test ride.

Does My Scooter Require a Motorcycle License Plate?

Regulations on this are different in every state, but anything that requires a motorcycle license will also require a motorcycle license plate. Riding without a plate can have severe consequences. As the popularity of scooters is on the increase, law-enforcement officials are wising up to the legal issues surrounding scooters. Scooterists may have passed their 150cc or larger scooters off as mopeds in the past, but it is unlikely to work much longer.

Not only is law enforcement getting information from the Department of Motor Vechicles (DMV), but officers also learn things when they pull over scooter riders and ask them questions about their bikes. Add to that the fact that police forces in major cities are incorporating scooters into their fleets. New York City, New Orleans, and St. Louis are noted for using scooters in tight urban spaces. As other police departments see the advantages of nimble vehicles with automatic transmissions, it is almost certain that many of them will adopt scooters for a variety of duties.

The era of ignorance about scooters on the part of law enforcement is drawing to a close. Most officers now know the basics of what defines a moped or motorized bicycle in their jurisdiction and how a motorcycle differs from that.

> **Kick Start**
>
> Your local office should be able to give you definitive information on registering your scooter. They should also be able to point you to motorcycle-related statutes and laws in your area.

DMV Info

Your local DMV should be able to give you proper information on how to go about registering your scooter, or point you to your state's statutes that regulate motorcycles and motorized bicycles or mopeds.

A few short years ago you could go into a local DMV office almost anywhere and get as many answers to your question as there were people working there. The sharp increase in scooter sales in that time has made more offices aware of the state and local registration issues for the areas they have jurisdiction over. Now if you go in to ask whether a certain make and model is eligible for registration as a moped or if it is even street legal, you are more likely to get a consistent and accurate answer than you would have 3 to 5 years ago.

Buying locally from a licensed dealer also really helps. In some states, the dealer is required to initiate the title transfer process on new vehicles. This removes one layer of hassle for you when purchasing a new scooter. Licensed dealers tend to have relationships with the local DMV office and the scooters they sell often are not scrutinized the same way that a mail-order scooter might be.

Do I Have to Wear a Helmet? Should I?

Thirty out of fifty U.S. states do not require adult motorcycle riders to wear helmets. It may not be legally required in many places, but it's still a good idea to wear one. Helmets are known to save lives and prevent head injuries, particularly in low-speed crashes.

Even if you don't legally have to wear a helmet, why would you not? Over the years, those who don't want to wear helmets have come up with many arguments for not doing it. They claim it will mess up their hair, but then again, so would crashing without a helmet. Wind also has a way of messing up your super cool hairdo. Others say that riding with a helmet looks dorky. Severe brain damage is a lot worse than looking dorky. The only excuse that really stands up at all is that some riders like feeling the wind on their faces and in their hair, which is quite silly because your hair will get messed up either way. It is an exhilarating way to ride, but riding with a half helmet or an open-face helmet provides much of the same sensation with vastly improved safety.

Wearing a helmet ties in with the idea of dressing to ride and being mentally prepared. It does help put your mind into riding mode and many find that it makes them more serious about the activity of riding.

A helmet is always a good idea, even if it's not required by law. Check with your local DMV about your state's laws.

(Photo by Bev Brinson)

Friends and family of William "Pete" Snell founded the Snell Memorial Foundation after he died in an auto-racing accident. His helmet did nothing to protect him from what should have been a survivable crash. The mission of the Snell Memorial Foundation is to "improve helmet design and capabilities, and to encourage the development and use of truly protective helmets." Their website contains great information on why to wear helmets and how to find the right one. They also have interesting news articles about developments in helmet technology.

Tips for Riding

The physical work of riding is actually not that hard. The mental work needed to get from point to point safely on two wheels is where you will expend the most energy.

There is a lot of sensory information to process. Keeping yourself in the proper frame of mind for riding makes you a safer rider. As part of your overall mental state, you need to be calm, aware, and undistracted. Distractions take too much of your mental energy away from observing your environment for potential hazards. When distracted, your awareness of your surroundings is seriously diminished. You may not notice an SUV making a left turn in front of you if you are busy thinking about the argument you just had with your significant other, or how much you hate your job, or if you're worried about a loved one in the hospital. When something that big is weighing on your mind, take the car. Only ride when you can focus entirely on riding. You need all your wits about you to stay alive.

One of the best things you can do is get in contact with the Motorcycle Safety Foundation and find out where and when you can take their courses. Their website can be found at www.msf-usa.org and their number is 1-800-446-9227. The MSF is known for their basic and intermediate rider courses, but they also recently began to offer courses in dirt and gravel riding. Though many may not consider that useful on a scooter, learning how to handle any kind of terrain is valuable as it broadens your riding skill set.

The key messages the MSF has for riders are the following: 1. Get trained and licensed. 2. Wear protective gear. 3. Ride unimpaired. 4. Ride within your limits. 5. Be a lifelong learner. All of these messages are very common-sense things, but many people do not follow them, particularly the advice about not riding impaired. According to a study by the National Highway Traffic Safety Administration, in half of all single-vehicle motorcycle accidents, the riders were intoxicated. Making the guidelines part of your riding philosophy will make you a safer and more skilled rider, with better odds of avoiding accidents, injuries, or death.

Dress to Ride

Dressing to ride is not as obvious on a scooter as it might be on a sport bike or a big cruiser. Though a full set of racing leathers might look like overkill on a scooter, it actually isn't. Most motorcycle accidents happen between 30 mph and 70 mph. Many scooters are capable of doing those speeds and what you fall off of does not matter to the pavement. At low speeds, protective gear can make the difference between a hospital visit and getting up and dusting yourself off. At higher speeds it increases the probability of surviving a crash and helps reduce the severity of injuries.

No matter what you choose to wear, it is important to be consistent with it. Getting dressed to ride becomes a ritual that helps mentally prepare you for a safe ride. If your ritual consists of putting on a helmet, then jacket, then gloves, you are telling your mind that it is time to ride. The more you see it that way, the less distracted you will be while riding.

Look Where You're Going—You'll Go Where You Look

Talk to any experienced riders and they could probably recount a tale of nearly hitting something that they could not stop looking at. And when a chair falls off the pickup truck in front of you with plenty of space to maneuver around it, you can't imagine how anyone could run into it.

def•i•ni•tion

> Target fixation is focusing on an object is getting fixated on a target. Typically this happens when a hazard presents itself. If a rider does not find a safe target to fix upon, a collision with the hazardous target is almost inevitable.

Target fixation is the reason why so many avoidable accidents occur. You see something, and you want to avoid it, so you keep looking at it and plan to move around it. However, the scooter wants to follow your eyes. The longer you look at it, the longer you will track toward it. Until you break your eyes away from what you're aiming at, you cannot really avoid it.

The best way to break your eyes away is to find something else to fix-ate upon. A spot ahead on the road is ideal. Fixating on something else gives you a new goal to ride toward. Because you will go where you look, your path will track away from the obstacle and toward the newly acquired target.

At some point it's important to stop fixating on targets and to keep tak-ing in visual information so you can ride safely. If you find yourself fix-ated on what appears to be an inevitable impact, redirecting can make all the difference.

This situation commonly presents itself on curves. When a straight road suddenly and sharply changes direction, it can be difficult to nego-tiate simply because you aren't looking where you want to go. A good riding habit to develop is to look at where you want to be in addition to looking at where you are.

Ride Defensively

The best riding advice I was ever given was, "Imagine you are invisible to everyone on the road, and act accordingly."

Most drivers are distracted by their audio systems, cell phones, bev-erages, and/or screaming offspring. It's often a wonder that they see the other cars on the road with them. Scooters are smaller and much harder to see. Coupled with the fact that cagers are not looking for anything the size or shape of you on your scooter, the practical reality is that you are invisible.

If you see a driver getting ready to make a left turn, you have to expect that he or she will not register your presence and will cut you off or hit you (the most common type of motorcycle accident involving multiple vehicles). In response, you have to be ready to brake, swerve, or do any-thing you can to avoid a collision. Most of the time, nothing will hap-pen. However, when someone does try to turn in front of you, you will be glad you were on the defensive.

It is also imperative to stay out of the blind spots of cars and trucks. When drivers do check their blind spots, they are typically only look-ing for other cars and trucks.

Oil Slick

Even if the driver makes eye contact with you, it does not mean that he or she "saw" you.

If they don't see a huge object looming next to them, the adjacent lane is assumed to be clear. Again, being prepared to rapidly accelerate, brake, swerve, or honk is critical. Eventually, you will find yourself at least somewhat able to anticipate the actions of the drivers around you. Even as you can judge threats, don't get cocky. Drivers around you will still do incredibly stupid or careless things without providing any warning signs at all.

Kick Start

Reflective items intended for bicyclists and joggers work well on scooters and are as close as a nearby sporting-goods store.

Make Yourself as Visible as Possible

Though it is assumed you will be invisible to those around you on the roads, there is a spectrum of invisibility. Bright, fluorescent colors, hyper-reflective materials, and the like can really make a difference, especially at night. If your chosen gear doesn't come in bright colors, an inexpensive day-glow reflective vest or some strategically placed strips of reflective tape can really make you stand out. Although being seen is no replacement for riding defensively, it does give you a small, but welcome, margin of safety.

When picking out a scooter, it doesn't hurt to have visibility in mind when you pick a color. Bright colors obviously stand out more than dark ones, particularly at dusk and later at night.

Even if you don't pick a brightly colored scooter, you can apply reflective vinyl to it if you are serious about being seen. Headlight modulators and brake flashers are another way to improve your visibility. Headlight modulators work while your high beam is active. A modulator will flash your headlight quickly, which many studies have shown increases the chance that drivers will see you. Motion is one of the things that the human eye is very good at detecting. On the other hand, there are studies that also show tendencies for drivers to focus on your headlight and have a target-fixation moment of their own.

Brake-light flashers are fairly self-descriptive. They flash your scooter's brake lights when you apply the brakes. Brightly flashing red lights are very hard to miss and will give you a bit of extra protection from being rear-ended.

Neon and LED accessory lighting may seem like accessories for the customization crowd, but they can actually increase the visibility of your scooter after dark. Every little bit helps, especially at night.

Wildlife

Encounters with animals are the cause of many single-vehicle motorcycle and scooter accidents.

Squirrels are known for being insane and running into the street in front of oncoming vehicles as though they have nothing to live for. The conventional wisdom in a car is not to swerve to miss most animals—the idea being that you are just as likely to lose control of the car and hit something more damaging than the animal who strayed into the path of your car. On a scooter, mass is not on your side like it is with a car. Even hitting small animals like squirrels can be a problem. If something gets caught in your front wheel it is likely to almost immediately stop the front wheel and catapult you over the headset of your scoot. Bigger animals like deer are dangerous to hit with cars, but on a scooter you don't have 1 to 2 tons of metal surrounding you.

> **Kick Start**
>
> Rural areas are not the only places where animals can put themselves on a collision course with you. As cities and suburbs have expanded, many animals like deer, foxes, raccoons, opossums, and others are now making homes within populated areas. Urban and suburban streets lacking streetlights should put you on alert after dark.

Generally, you are better off avoiding any collision you can when riding on two wheels. Your scooter should be more nimble and agile than your car, and, as such, you have better chances of avoiding obstacles that jump into your path.

A key to accident avoidance is awareness. Just as you may develop a strong intuition about the cars around you and when one might unexpectedly cut you off, you can also learn to recognize places where wildlife are prevalent. Residential streets lined with mature oak trees are likely to have scores of squirrels chasing one another through the street. In that environment it's important to be ready at all times to brake or swerve with little notice.

Along roads through wooded areas or near farm fields and pastures, it's important to look for deer, especially around dusk and during the evening. Be on the alert for round reflections along the roadside. Riding with your high beam on helps you see farther and it illuminates the height of a deer's eyes. If you do spot a reflection you should slow down immediately. If you pass a deer, don't speed up immediately, as there are almost certainly several more very close by.

Dogs may not be considered wildlife, but they have been known to cause riding accidents. When approaching a dog it's a good idea to slow down to be sure you can get around the dog. As you approach the dog, speed up quickly; it often makes them lose interest in chasing after you. Attempting to kick at a dog is more likely to make you lose control of your scooter than it is to scare the dog away.

Practice Makes Habit

Practicing your riding skills in a controlled environment is one of the most valuable activities you can do on your scooter. Knowing how to properly execute a panic stop when asked and actually doing it with adrenaline pumping through you are two very different things. Other physical activities, like sports or dancing, require practice to master the techniques required to be good at them, and so does riding. Correctly training in emergency-riding maneuvers develops muscle memory that will serve you in an actual emergency. The goal is to get to the point of not having to consciously think about every detail of panic braking or swerving to avoid an animal or object in the road. The more you do practice the correct methods, the safer you will be out on the open roads.

> **Kick Start**
>
> If looking for a place to practice, your criteria should include a minimum of traffic, smooth pavement, and open spaces without obstacles like light poles and curbs close at hand.

Training is not just for novices; even veteran riders should go out and refresh their skills periodically to keep them honed to a razor's edge. Practicing with other riders is a good way to get feedback on your riding habits and to see how others may do things a little differently than you do.

Weather—And How to Adjust Your Riding for Different Conditions

Smart drivers know that driving in snow is completely different than on dry pavement. Smart riders learn quickly that, because they have only half the wheels of a car, being aware of conditions is even more vital. If you're out when snow starts falling or if it gets icy, you need to get home quickly or get somewhere you can safely leave your scoot. Riding on snow and ice is something that most veteran riders won't do, and novices most definitely need not apply for it.

Riding in cold weather can be problematic. If you're riding at temperatures below freezing, you have to be very aware that there could be black ice out on the roads that you won't see. It often forms along the edges of roads, as well as in dips and potholes. If you live in a particularly dry climate, low temperatures alone might not be a problem, but it's still something to be on the lookout for.

The other cold-weather factor to keep in mind is wind chill. Riding is a human-made wind chill that you selectively apply. If you aren't properly attired, you are going to get extremely cold. In addition to the very real possibility of frostbite, you also get distracted and fatigued much more quickly in the cold than you do in nice weather. Some riders have also found that their muscles get so tensed up when cold that they have trouble loosening their hands from the grips and using their fingers to pull the brake and clutch levers. Steering also becomes difficult when your arms tighten up.

Though riding in the rain is not particularly pleasant, it can be done safely. You should not ride during the first 10 minutes of a rain, so that you can allow the oils and dust to be washed off the pavement. Combined with water, those items make the roads extremely slick. As they wash away, the road still is slippery but much less so. Riding slowly in the rain is important. Your braking distances are worsened, and you cannot lean as much through the corners. Judicious and gentle use of the throttle is also really important, particularly when exiting a turn.

Even though riding in the center of a lane is usually recommended, riding in the tire tracks of the other cars on the road is often recommended in rainy conditions. Oil, antifreeze, and other slick and nasty stuff tend to gather in the center of the road. Though much of it will rinse away, some of it does not, and the center of a wet road is usually the slipperiest part. Painted areas of the pavement also tend to become slippery when wet. The large blocks and lettering around crosswalks really tend to be the worst. Be cautious about turning, braking, and applying throttle when in the proximity of that kind of danger. Manhole covers and other metal road fixtures are also extremely perilous. Even the ones with texture still become extremely slick when doused with water. The large steel plates used in construction areas should also be avoided, or taken with extreme caution for the same reason.

Rain can cause road conditions to change quickly. It's a good idea to watch the forecast.

After the rain there can be other treacherous obstacles to safely navigate. Wet leaves are a common fall occurrence in many parts of North America. Wet leaves have a tendency to slide around on top of one another. They also tend to build up at side-street intersections. Taking off from a stop, particularly if turning, can be hair-raising when it feels like the road is sliding out from under your rear tire.

Other road conditions need to influence your riding style as well. Sand, choppy pavement, or grooved roads should really slow you down and make you more cautious.

The Least You Need to Know

- *Helmets save lives.*
- Follow the same laws you would in your car.
- To avoid accidents, look where you want to go.
- Ride as though nobody can see you.
- Watch for wildlife.
- Slow down for bad weather and obstacles.

Chapter 5

Basic Maintenance

In This Chapter

- Common scooter maintenance requirements
- Taking care of your tires
- Easy upkeep you can do yourself
- When to let a pro handle it

Like any other machine, a scooter will require some care to keep it running smoothly. Problems that would be merely annoyances on four wheels can become hazardous to life and limb when they occur on two wheels.

In this chapter we will cover some basic maintenance requirements. Though many of them will be discussed in detail, this chapter is in no way intended to be a repair manual or an all-encompassing or definitive guide to repairing your scooter. Instead, look at it as a general outline of the repairs and maintenance to expect your machine to need. If you decide that the jobs seem like something you can handle, find a shop manual, get out the toolbox, and have at it. If you decide that the tasks described are a bit over your head, you will at least have a good idea of what services you are paying for when you take your scooter in for repair work.

Tires

Tires literally are where the rubber meets the road. They are important to the ride, handling, braking, and safety of any vehicle. However, there is much more at stake on two wheels than four. Veteran riders will tell you to treat your tires as though your life depends on them, because it does.

Monitor tire wear and avoid a blowout.

(Photo by Bev Brinson)

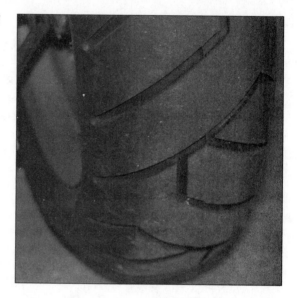

Checking Pressure

Monitoring your tire pressure is one of the most overlooked mainte-nance items. It's also the easiest and cheapest. A tire-pressure gauge costs a couple of bucks, and will fit in most scooters. Check the pres-sure once a week at a minimum before you have ridden and heated up the tires. Also vital is to inflate to the scooter manufacturer's recom-mended pressure; it is the proper pressure for the handling and ride characteristics the factory intended. The number on the tire only tells the maximum pressure rating of the tire. Appropriately inflated tires will make your scooter handle better and ride more comfortably, shorten braking distances, and should get you better mileage.

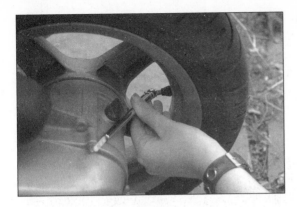

A tire-pressure gauge is an invaluable tool.

(Photo by Bev Brinson)

Tires that are not inflated to the proper pressure will make a scooter have strange handling, poor ride quality, and lower fuel economy. Moreover, underinflated tires will get odd wear patterns that can ruin them quickly. Scooter tires may not last very long, but with the price that some of them command, it can get very expensive not to perform the simple task of keeping them inflated.

Overinflated tires generally have a stiffer ride than those inflated to the recommended pressure. Moderately going over the maximum pressure can be acceptable if you are carrying heavy items or a passenger. Going overboard causes problems. Odd wear patterns can happen with over-inflation and the ride generally becomes stiffer. Extremely excessive pressures can put undue stress on the tire. Unless you're experienced at figuring out what pressure to use, things will be better if you just stick to the manufacturer's recommendations.

Checking Tread Wear

Looking at your tire treads to see what kind of shape they are in is another overlooked yet simple maintenance item. You will be able to tell easily when your tread is becoming worn. The outer edges tend to stay in good shape much longer than the center. Compare the crown of the tire to the edges.

You should also be looking for uneven wear. This is a sign that something is wrong with your scoot. It could be as simple as tire pressure, or something more serious. Loose steering head bearings, bent forks, and bad wheel bearings can cause tire wear that is not uniform.

Keeping up on your tires helps you stay in the know about the general health of your machine. Scooter tires only tend to last 3,000 to 6,000 miles depending on diameter, width, and rubber compound. Sporty tires with high levels of grip tend to wear out much faster than harder compounds, but all should be looked at frequently. Checking your tread wear every day takes virtually no time at all, but it keeps you abreast of the general health of your scooter.

Changing Tires

Eventually your tires will wear out and need replacement. Typically the rear tire will go first. Most manual-shift scooters make changing tires very easy. The single-sided fork the Vespas, Stellas, and Bajaj scooters use was designed with fast roadside tire changes in mind. The intent was to be able to quickly remove a tire and replace it with a spare. The rear tire also unbolts in a similar manner to the front.

After removing the wheel, manual-shift scooters have another trick up their sleeve. The rim separates to make putting on a new tire a very quick and simple process. After letting the air out of the tire, unbolt the rim halves and separate them. You can then put in new tubes and mount the new tire. After bolting everything back together, you inflate the tire and reinstall it onto the scooter.

On automatic scooters the process is a bit more complicated. Most automatics use conventional motorcycle forks up front. Removing the axle bolt is pretty simple, but it's very important to make note of the order of the spacers and pieces. When reassembled, it's important that they are all there and installed in the proper position. Removing the rear wheel can be a little more difficult. On most automatics the exhaust pipe has to be removed for the sake of access. After doing that, you have to remove the cotter pin, the cap over the central nut, and finally the central nut. The difficulty in the last part is that the wheel and axle will spin as you try to loosen the nut. The wheel has to be held firmly in place while you loosen the nut. An impact wrench makes very quick work of removing the nut without even having to secure the rear wheel.

Once the front or rear wheel is off, the difficult part has just begun. Modern scooters nearly always use tubeless tires. The basic concept of tubeless tires makes the use of a split rim basically impossible.

To change out the tire you need to be able to clamp down the wheel and then use specialized tools to remove the deflated wheel. Without the proper tools it's a task that often brings on a lot of swearing and tool throwing.

The easy way to handle a tubeless tire change is to take the removed wheel into your scooter shop or a motorcycle mechanic and have the new tire mounted there. Though many scooters don't really need to have their wheels and tires spin-balanced, it doesn't hurt to have it done. On some scooters it seems to be helpful. Owners of larger big-wheel scooters often claim a noticeable difference between balanced and unbalanced wheels. A few owners of the Vespa GT200 have made the same observations. The labor charge to have your new tires mounted is usually reasonable if you remove the wheels yourself and take them into the shop. It's cheaper than buying the proper tools and throwing them across the garage when the task becomes difficult.

When putting the wheels back on, it's very important to put everything back just as it was. A torque wrench is valuable to have when tightening everything back down. Under-tightening can cause fasteners to vibrate loose at very inopportune times. Wheel or suspension-related fasten-ers coming loose or falling off can easily put you into a world of pain. Excessively tightening the fasten-ers can strip them or cause them to break, which will leave you without a scooter until you can get the fas-tener repaired. As with all repairs, do not attempt this task if you do not have the proper tools or if you are not mechanically inclined.

Oil Slick _____

Often there are peculiari-ties to scooter repair that go against conventional repair methods for cars or motor-cycles. So always read the instructions thoroughly before attempting any repair or service.

Oil

Oil is the lifeblood of most machines. Without it, things come to a screeching halt. It is one of the most obvious maintenance issues of any machine. If you take care of your scooter's lubrication needs, it should reward you with a long life free of catastrophic failures.

Good quality 2-stroke oil is sold in scooter and motorcycle shops.

(Photo by Bev Brinson)

Two-Stroke Oil

Two-strokes operate on a total-loss principle. You put two-stroke oil in the oil tank and it gets automatically mixed with fuel (scooters without autolube systems require you to mix the oil and fuel directly) and run through the engine. Unlike a four-stroke, you don't need to change the engine oil, because it changes itself. Check the oil level in the tank every time you fuel up to be sure you have enough. Running the oil tank dry will cause your engine to seize, which will at the very least require a new piston and cylinder. More seriously, it could also damage your crankshaft.

Having a little oil always on board your scooter is a great idea. You're probably thinking that you can buy two-stroke oil at your local discount retailer. While you can, it's almost guaranteed to be oil for weed whackers, chainsaws, and other garden equipment. Lawn-equipment two-stroke oil is not intended for use in motor-vehicle engines, and should not go into your scooter. Lawn equipment is designed to run at an idle speed and an operating speed. As such, it can use oils that are not as protective over a wide range of engine speeds and under the kind of loads that a laden scooter puts on an engine. Bring at least a little bit of good-quality two-stroke oil along with you on your scooter at all times. Next time you run low on oil, you may be a long way from home or a retailer that sells motorcycle two-stroke oil.

Spending a little extra for a motorcycle-specific synthetic oil is cheaper than getting a rebuilt or new engine. This is especially true if you have performance-enhancing modifications on your scoot.

Generally, it's best to use the automatic oiling system on a stock scooter. Premixing your fuel and oil instead of using the oil-injection system is usually recommended when you begin tuning your engine for more performance. It's also important to realize that on a two-stroke, lubrication is dependent upon throttle usage. On downhill runs it's good to blip the throttle occasionally to keep your engine oiled so it won't seize up. This is really important on manual-shift scooters when they are left in gear, to provide engine-braking down a steep grade. They can heat up quite quickly in hilly terrain if you don't do your part as the rider to keep the engine lubed.

> ### Scootrivia
>
> For those who find their exhaust gasses too bland or offensive, strawberry-scented two-stroke oil can sweeten things up a bit.

Four-Stroke Oil

Rather like a car, it's good to check the oil level every other time you fill up. On a scooter, it's even more important, because the oil capacity is so small that being a bit low can harm your engine if left unchecked.

The typical procedure for checking your oil is to do so with the engine on the stand. Remove the dipstick (often it's built into the filler cap), wipe it off, and reinsert it. If it is built into the filler cap, you typically need to screw the cap back on to get the dipstick to the place where it will read accurately. If the oil level is low, be cautious when adding oil. Too much oil can really damage an engine, usually by creating high-enough pressures to make oil seals pop out of place.

It definitely is a pain to check the oil, fill a little bit, and check again until full. However, it's less annoying and less painful to your wallet than having an oil seal burst and to see your scooter puke oil everywhere. It's also less painful than having your scooter sling oil onto your rear tire, causing you to lose traction and crash. With a little practice, you will get an idea of how much oil needs to be added just by looking at the dipstick reading.

Oil and filter changes are necessary like they are on a car, and you should follow the manufacturer's maintenance schedule. This is a task that a mechanically inclined individual could undertake if armed with a good owner's manual and a small set of metric tools.

The basic process is to fully drain the oil and remove the filter. Replace the filter with a new one, replace the drain plug, and refill with oil. The reality of it can be a bit trickier. All of those tasks must be accomplished for a successful oil change, but on many scooters, the center stand can complicate the job. When feeding a baby, it's unbelievable how such a small amount of food can turn into such a big mess. It's similarly astounding how the small volume of oil can yield such a big mess.

It is expected that most repair shops doing oil changes will have a motorcycle lift. With a lift, the stand does not need to be down for the bike to stay up. Drainage that flows unimpeded without a stand in the way can trickle down to the ground if the scooter is on the motorcycle lift. For easy cleanup, park over a big piece of cardboard. Also find a few small funnels at the store before doing the job. The more you can direct the used oil away from the center stand, the less cleanup you will have to do. A big roll of shop paper towels comes in handy during this job.

Kick Start

There are many types of oils available, and their relative merits are the subject of great debate. Generally it does not matter which brand you use as long as it is the weight and grade specified in your owner's manual. Synthetics can be used in engines that don't call for them, but nonsynthetic oil should not be used in engines that require synthetic.

Some scooters do not use conventional spin-on filters, which screw onto the engine. Most Kymco four-strokes, for example, use a special screen that catches sludge. During an oil change it gets cleaned out and put back in the scooter. No new oil filter to buy. The flip side is that the oil needs to be changed more frequently.

Gear and Hub Oil

While engines need oil, there are other parts that need lubrication for smooth operation. On automatic scooters the rear-wheel hub system usually has a small reservoir of oil. Many manufacturers specify a 6,000-mile interval for changing it. On some scooters this is a service that a mechanically adept owner could handle; on others it's more a more involved procedure.

Manual-shift scoots have oil to lubricate the transmission, which should be changed at the mileage the manufacturer recommends.

You may not notice where the gear oil is, but once you do note it, it's very obvious.

(Photo by Bev Brinson)

The procedure for changing these oils is basically the same as changing the oil on a four-stroke, except gearboxes and axle hubs usually do not have oil filters. Open the drain plug, then the fill cap, and let the oil drain. Be very careful to make sure it does not get onto your rear tire. Refill the transmission or hub carrier with the proper grade and weight of lubricant specified by the manufacturer.

As with a four-stroke engine, too much oil is a bad thing. Do not over-fill as this can lead to oil-seal problems. On some automatic scooters, overfilling has caused oil to end up on the automatic clutch. Automatic-scooter clutches are supposed to stay dry. Covering the clutch with oil will cause it to no longer work properly.

If your scooter has a hub or transmission dipstick, be sure to check it before riding around. If it does not have a dipstick then you need to measure out the specified amount of oil to pour in.

Some scooters have the drain plug in a spot that is only accessible with the wheel removed. If your scooter is like that, then you should leave the wheel off until you know for sure that you have filled the case with the proper amount of oil. Having to remove the wheel again to drain a little bit of oil off would be quite a hassle.

Brakes

Unless you are mechanically competent and somewhat experienced at working on your own vehicles, a safety item like brakes is often best left to professionals, or to be done under the guidance of a knowledge-able person. The consequences of screwing up something engine-related generally just mean you will need a new engine. Screwing up a brake job can end in a trip to the emergency room.

Disc Brakes

Brake pads will need to be replaced periodically, but how often depends a lot on your use. If most of your braking is progressive and gentle, yours will probably last longer than if you use them hard. Mileage has little to do with brake use. Ten miles of stop-and-go traffic will wear your brakes more than fifty miles of cruising along with only a few stops. At some point the hydraulic system should have its fluid flushed and refilled because brake fluid absorbs water over time, which reduces its effectiveness. This service is not a frequent one, however. Rotor discs also need to be checked for thickness, cracks, and warping. When in for a 3,000- or 6,000-mile service, these items should be inspected.

A front disc brake illustrates where the brake pad grabs the disc.

(Photo by Bev Brinson)

If you have inspected everything and determined that you only need a new set of brake pads, it's a pretty easy job. Unbolt the front caliper from the fork or the rear-axle hub carrier. With the caliper free, spread the brake pads apart. The caliper's hydraulic pistons should retract into the housing. If they don't, consider taking the scooter to a shop that can do the work for you.

With the pistons compressed, you can remove the brake pads. Every manufacturer fastens them in differently. Some calipers use pins, others employ tabs, and a few even use spring-tension clips to secure the pads in position. With the old brake pads off you can use brake-parts cleaner spray to clean everything up. Unless your manual prohibits it, you can also sparingly apply anti-squeak compound between the new brake pads and the pistons to prevent squeal when stopping. Be sure not to get this onto the friction surface of the pad or onto your brake rotor. It will cause your brakes to be less effective. With the new pads in place, the caliper can be bolted back onto the fork or to the hub carrier. This is another place where having a torque wrench is good for peace of mind, and for being able to easily remove the fasteners during the next brake job.

Flushing and refilling the brake system is another job that needs to happen at periodic intervals, but they are very long. This is a process that should only be attempted by professional mechanics or highly skilled and mechanically experienced owners. If all of the air is not bled from the hydraulic system, the brakes will be much less effective and will often not work when needed most.

Drum Brakes

Drum brakes have curved shoes instead of the flat pads of a disc-brake system. Brake shoes press against a rotating metal drum to stop the wheel. These also will need to be replaced periodically. Just like brake pads, brake life is determined by usage, not by mileage.

Changing brake shoes is slightly more difficult than replacing brake pads, but well within reach of an owner who does not shy away from being called a shade-tree mechanic. The process starts with removing the wheel. Once that is removed and there is access to the shoes, they can be removed. New ones can then be installed. As all of them are a little different, specifics won't be covered here. Look to your repair manual for specific guidance on how to properly do the job.

Before putting everything back together, perform a preliminary adjustment to the rods and cables as outlined in your manual. Final adjustment of the lever cable can occur once the wheel is back on your scooter. Periodically, these cables will also need to be adjusted. On most scooters there is a knob to carry out this adjustment. On some older scooters there are bolts or nuts that need to be loosened before the cable can be drawn tight. Once adequately taut, the bolt or nut can be tightened.

Carburetor Cleaning

With daily use, your *carburetor* isn't likely to need cleaning. Over time, gasoline gets gummy and will sometimes contain impurities. If your scooter sits around for a long period of time, or if you frequent a rather dodgy gas station, your carburetor may need to be cleaned. Usually this means removing it from the engine, disassembling it, and soaking it in carburetor cleaner. Compressed air is often used to blast out little bits of gunk. If you know how to do this, and how to properly reassemble the

def•i•ni•tion

The **carburetor** is a device that mixes air and fuel at the proper ratio. It also controls the engine speed.

carburetor, it's a fairly simple job. If you don't know what you're doing then this job should be left to those with experience. There are several small pieces that need to go back in properly for everything to work.

One simple thing that you can do even if you're not quite up to the task of disassembling and cleaning your carburetor is removing the hose that runs to the air-filter housing. With the hose out of the way, you can then open the throttle plate and spray carburetor cleaner around inside the carburetor. This is a good thing to try out before going to the trouble of removing the carburetor and tearing it down. If you are lucky, it may solve your problems. If your scooter has been sitting an inordinate amount of time, a simple spray-down with carburetor cleaner may not be enough, particularly if the jets are plugged up with gunk.

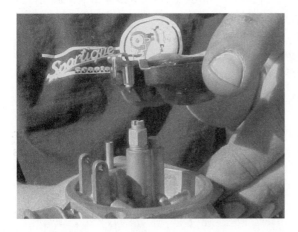

A carburetor bowl, ready to be cleaned by a mechanic at Sportique Scooters of Denver.

(Photo by Bev Brinson)

Oil Slick

Carburetor and choke-cleaner products can be hazardous. Always wear eye protection when working with spray solvents. Carburetor cleaner in the eyes is a painful experience that we do not recommend.

Cleaning the Air Filter

This is another simple maintenance item. Removing the filter is typically no more complicated than removing six to ten screws to detach the air-box cover.

On many scooters, the filter is an oiled foam element and gets washed, oiled, and reinstalled. Usually you just wash the element in warm, soapy water. Wringing it out several times and working water and soap into it helps get all the dust and junk out of the filter. Rinsing it in clean water helps ready it for the oiling process. Once all the grime and soap are rinsed out, let the filter dry out before adding oil. Some manufacturers have specific oils they want used. Others recommend the normal motor oil. Most suggest using just a little bit of oil, because the crankcase breather system will add oil to the filter. Follow the manufacturer's guidelines closely. If too much oil is added, it can cause the filter to flow less freely than it should, which will weaken performance.

Disposable paper elements are also commonly used for engine filtration. If you have a replacement part in hand, they are very easy to change. The process is usually less time-consuming than washing out a foam filter. It is a little more costly, though. Many manufacturers recommend that filters be replaced or cleaned around the same time as replacing the drive belt and roller weights.

Air filters are easy to access and clean.

(Photo by Bev Brinson)

Adjusting the Idle

As the temperature changes, the idle speed can become too fast or slow. On most automatic scooters there is a small plug in the underseat bucket. With the plug removed, the idle-adjustment screw becomes accessible. On modern manual-shift scooters the engine cowl needs to be removed for access. The typical procedure is to warm up the engine and then adjust the idle speed. The screw should be turned slowly to allow the engine to respond to changes.

Scooter makers often have a specific rpm they recommend for an idle speed, but without a tachometer it's often hard to tell. There are aftermarket digital tachometers that are useful for setting idle speeds. However, unless you're going to also use it for performance tuning, it's a bit expensive for just adjusting the idle a few times a year. The amateur method is to set the idle speed to one that feels comfortable. It should not be so slow that it feels like it will stall, but it should not be too fast, either. On an automatic, the idle is too high if the clutch starts to engage. If you can feel the clutch grabbing and the bike trying to tug forward while stopped and not holding the brakes, then the idle speed needs to be reduced. After riding for a long period of time you will know exactly where to adjust it to have it feel normal.

Replacing Spark Plugs

Cars today often have 100,000-mile spark-plug change intervals. Scooters do not. The interval varies greatly by manufacturer. Two-strokes also tend to need replacement a bit more often than four-strokes, but you can count on an interval somewhere between 6,000 and 12,000 miles.

Spark-plug replacement on most scooters is a simple task, assuming the plug is easy to get to. If the plug is readily accessible, all that needs to be done is to remove the plug wire, put a spark-plug socket on the plug, and loosen it. If the plug is not easy to get to, then you may have to unbolt the engine from the shock to pivot it into a position where you can access the plug. When installing a new plug, it's really important to twist it in gently. It is far too easy to cross-thread spark plugs if you aren't being very careful and sensitive. If the plug isn't threading smoothly, its binding and pressure will only mess up the threads on the cylinder head. Once it threads in completely by hand, you can then tighten it with the plug socket again.

Checking the Drive Belt for Wear

The rubber belts on automatic scooters are consumable items in much the same way that tires are. They have a life expectancy somewhere between 4,000 and 8,000 miles. Kevlar-reinforced belts are available and usually last longer than stock ones.

To check belt wear you have to measure it. If there are no signs of damage and the belt is within specifications, it can stay. Often, it makes more sense to just have the belt changed because of the labor involved in getting in there.

An example of a good-quality drive belt.

(Photo by Bev Brinson)

To get to the belt, you typically have to remove the transmission cover. It's a pretty simple task. Usually there are a series of bolts around the perimeter. Some scooters also run the nut for the rear-clutch shaft through the belt cover, but many do not. If your scooter does have the clutch shaft poking through, you will also need to remove the nut. To do this, you will either need an impact wrench or some way of locking up the clutch shaft.

With the belt cover off, you may be able to measure the belt without removing the variator pulley. If you cannot, you will have to lock up the variator shaft or use an impact wrench. As mentioned earlier, if you have gone this far or need to replace roller weights, you might as well just replace the belt along with it. The variator pulley does have to come off to replace the belt, so it takes only a moment or so to wiggle a new belt into place.

Kick Start

Special tools are available for some models to lock the variator and clutch shafts. Locking the clutch shaft on some models also locks up the rear wheel, which will make it easier to remove that as well.

Reassembly is the reverse of disassembly, as they say. A torque wrench is important on rotating components like the variator and clutch shaft. If those nuts loosen, then they can cause very expensive damage to the CVT and to the crankshaft output shaft.

Any time you are in the CVT housing, it's a good idea to remove any of the dust deposits that come from the clutch.

Inspecting and Replacing Roller Weights

When the belt is checked, the rollers are typically inspected and often replaced. Over time they develop flat spots and no longer actually roll. Consequently your acceleration and top speed suffer. The part cost of a new set of rollers is low enough that it makes more sense to just replace them, given the labor involved.

Changing the roller weights starts out like changing the belt. The CVT cover is removed, and then the variator pulley is taken off. After pulling out the belt, the second half of the variator pulley comes out. There are usually a few spacers behind it. Be sure to note the order they are in, as they need to go back in the same way they came out. Once that half is out, the roller weights can be removed from it and new ones can be put in. With that half put back in, a new belt can be installed as described above.

Adjusting and Replacing Cables

Adjusting cables is a fairly straightforward process. Usually they will need to be tightened rather than loosened. As noted in the drum-brake section, most modern cables have adjustment knobs. Modern manual scooters have an older design that requires loosening a bolt and adjusting the cables. Though not quite as simple as a modern brake cable, it's certainly not out of reach for the mechanically inclined owner with a good manual.

The Least You Need to Know

- ◆ Check your tire pressure weekly.
- ◆ Always use your owner's manual.
- ◆ Briefly inspect your scooter before every ride.
- ◆ Keeping your scooter in tip-top condition keeps you safe.

Chapter 6

Storing Your Scooter

In This Chapter

- ◆ Scooter hibernation
- ◆ Keeping your battery healthy
- ◆ Pre-storage maintenance
- ◆ Deterring thieves

If you are not hardy enough for winter riding or your local conditions make it impossible, your scooter will need to be stored. Following are tips to help your scooter start right up after storage.

Battery Charging

Batteries need to be cared for in order to live a long life. Cold temperatures are rough on batteries and shorten life. To properly care for a battery over an extended period of not using it, you need to keep it warm and charged. Bring your battery inside and keep it on the tender while your scooter is hibernating, or just hook it up for a couple of days a month. Small cat-litter trays can make great containers for batteries, especially batteries that aren't of the sealed "maintenance-free" variety. If your battery isn't sealed, this is also a good time to check and top off the fluid level.

> **Oil Slick**
>
> Be very careful about how you charge your battery. A battery charger should not be left on the battery at all times, but a tender with a float mode can be. It is also very important to be sure you have the positive and negative leads attached to the correct terminals. Improperly charging a battery can cause hazardous gas fumes to build up, and in some cases it can even cause explosions.

There is often confusion about how to maintain your battery. Do you need a charger? Do you need an automatic battery tender? Some chargers are not intended to be left on a battery and will eventually overcharge it. This can boil off the electrolyte in the battery. Excess heat and explosive gasses are also consequences of overcharging a battery. Basic chargers that do not have float-mode monitoring need to be manually managed. High-amp quick chargers also are not recommended on small batteries for the same reasons.

Automatic battery-tending devices can charge up your battery and keep it charged. Most of them have float-mode monitoring capabilities. When the battery is sufficiently charged, the device no longer charges the battery. When it senses storage being down in the battery, it then begins to charge until it's full again. Some of these products can be used while the battery is still installed. Many of them even come with pigtail connectors that screw down onto the battery terminals. Charging up is as quick and easy as plugging in the connector to the battery terminals, and then plugging into the wall. A charger with that feature makes life easier for those who ride short distances in cold weather.

Fancy charging gadgets are also available that have modes to warm the battery in winter and to periodically strip sulfates off the internal battery electrodes for improved battery longevity. Many of these also have some weatherproofing and can be used outdoors. Improved safety features are also common on more expensive chargers that will not allow them to operate with the positive and negative leads put on the incorrect battery terminals.

A battery charger is key to getting your battery through a cold winter. This one from CTEK does the job with ease.

(Photo courtesy of CTEK)

Kick Start

If you don't plan to ride your scooter for a month, it's a good idea to do some preventative care on your fuel system so it will start right up when you start riding again. Failure to do so can require removing and cleaning the carburetor or other fuel-system components.

Protecting the Fuel System

Gasoline tends to gum up and become less useful over time. As this happens, it can get the fuel system dirty, especially when a scooter is being stored. There are two schools of thought on how to prevent this problem from happening. One says to completely empty the fuel system; the other says to add a fuel stabilizer. One of the fortunate things about most modern scooters is that they have plastic gas tanks, which will obviously never rust or otherwise corrode. On a modern scooter, either method should work quite well.

Storing Dry

The dry method is just as it sounds. The tank, the carburetor, and all fuel hoses are completely empty. Basically, the idea is to drain as much gas as possible from the tank to empty the carburetor. There are two methods, both of which require a reasonable amount of work.

To drain the system, you will need to get the gas out of the tank. On a scooter with a manually operated fuel valve, you turn the valve to off. Then remove the hose from the carburetor that goes to the tank. Open the valve and drain away into an approved container.

Automatic scooters usually have vacuum-operated fuel valves. The hose is disconnected, but then the vacuum hose is also disconnected. A small, hand-operated vacuum pump is sufficient to open the valve to allow the fuel to drain into the previously mentioned approved container.

With the tank empty, you can then focus on the carburetor. There should be a screw and a drain hose that allows the fuel in the carburetor to drain out. With those tasks accomplished, your fuel system is drained. Reconnect all hoses so you don't forget to do it later.

As an alternative, some people just run their fuel tanks dry and let the scoot completely run out of gas. There are some claims that this is harmful, while others say it's completely harmless. On fuel-injected scooters it should not be done because it can cause damage to the fuel pump, replacement of which tends to be costly.

If a scooter won't be ridden for years, or indefinitely, a dry fuel system may be the best way to go. A dry tank is almost universally required when shipping a scooter or motorcycle, so it's a good thing to have an idea of how to do it. For only a short season of hibernation, the stabilizer method is much easier and comparable in result.

Adding Fuel Stabilizer

There are a number of *fuel stabilizers* on the market, and a quick jaunt to your local auto parts store will open your eyes to a world of products intended to prevent your gasoline from turning into sludgy varnish.

Though procedures may differ from product to product, it's pretty common to have very little gas in the tank when adding the stabilizer. Use the proper amount of stabilizer to treat the number of gallons in the tank. After putting in the stabilizer, the tank is then filled up with fuel.

> **def•i•ni•tion**
>
> A **fuel stabilizer** is a chemical compound in liquid form that reduces the volatility of gasoline, allowing it to be stored for long periods of time.

It's a good idea to swish your scooter side to side to mix the stabilizer and fuel. Then you typically run it for a little bit to get the treated fuel into the entirety of the fuel system. A trip around the block will mix the fuel and stabilizer and run it through the entire fuel system.

Adding stabilizer is the preferred method for fuel-injected scooters, because running them dry is damaging to expensive components of the injection system. There are a number of small passages for fuel in the injection system that might not go completely dry and would still gum up. Stabilizing the fuel as described should do the job.

Oil

Over the course of a riding season, a four-stroke scooter will get some fuel and contaminants in the oil. These can cause corrosion and damage to sensitive parts of the engine. It's a really good idea to change your oil before storing your scooter for an extended period of time. Some owners also swear by changing the oil before riding again, but this is often regarded as overkill.

Extremely extended periods of storage require more involved oiling procedures. Not only should one change the oil, but it's also a good idea to add some oil to the cylinder itself via the spark-plug hole. This is done to coat the cylinder wall with oil so it will not rust or otherwise corrode while the engine is not being used for years at a time. The same can be done with two-stroke oil to the cylinder walls of two-stroke engines.

Tires

Proper inflation will really help keep your tires in excellent shape. Tires have a way of losing air, particularly in colder conditions. As a tire softens and bends, some of those bends can become almost permanent creases. Over time, flat spots can develop on whichever tire is touching the ground. Periodically make sure that the tires are inflated to the scooter manufacturer's recommended pressure. It can save you some money down the road on replacing your scoot's shoes.

Though you may want to shine up your tires, you should never do it under any circumstances on a two-wheeler. Imagine trying to ride after slathering your tires with petroleum jelly. Applying tire-shine compounds is roughly equivalent. The shine doesn't last particularly long, and any cool points you might score for having slick-looking tires will be forfeited if you crash.

Washing Your Scooter

Hosing your scooter down is a regular part of general upkeep. Before putting it away for an extended period of time, giving your scoot a thorough cleaning is highly recommended. A trip to the self-service car wash is one way to go. The convenience is hard to beat. Having soap, a spray wand, and spot-free rinse water all at hand with virtually no cleanup is quite appealing.

Conversely, there are a few things to avoid. The high-pressure setting should be used with extreme caution. Spraying it into the wrong place can drive water into electrical connectors or sensitive mechanical systems. If you do choose to use it, do so from several feet away and be sure not to aim into cracks or places where there is wiring.

The automotive soap is just fine, but many of the other specialty sprays shouldn't go on your scooter. If you really wish to get that glossy shine with a fresh coat of wax, you're better off doing it by hand than you are using the spray. Wax should only go on the smooth and shiny panels and not onto matte or textured plastics, and working by hand helps prevent wax buildup where it shouldn't be. If wax and other sprays get onto your tires they can seriously reduce grip and set you up for an accident on your freshly cleaned scooter. Spot-free rinses are usually okay. Afterward it's a good idea to use a chamois cloth to dry off your scooter.

For old-school types who prefer a simple hose and a bucket, the same advice as above applies. It's better to use automotive soap, because dish soap can be harsh on paint. It's also inadvisable to use ammonia or ammonia-based cleaners on your plastics. If they are painted, those chemicals can ruin your paint. Even if they aren't, it can do some nasty things to plastic. If you do have unpainted or clear plastics that have dulled, there are special plastic polishes that are available at most auto-parts stores. These should not be used on paint because they can wear through the paint or dull it.

Taking measures to protect the material covering of your seat is a good idea. However, it's important to pick the right product. Sliding around the saddle while braking, accelerating, or cornering is not safe and not much fun. A protectant product for vinyl that isn't intended for shine is one of the ways to go. Wiping down excess before riding and letting it absorb is also wise. For scooters with leather seats, there are a number of products that are designed to protect and condition leather to keep it soft. Most will not have the sliding-around side effect that many vinyl products do.

Metal polishing products are also wonderful for keeping the bright metals shiny and gleaming. It's important to know that not all of the shiny metal on your scooter is chrome. Some of it may be aluminum that has been polished and possibly anodized. Be sure to check the labels of the metal products before using them. Some are meant specifically for certain metals and finishes, and should not really be used on others.

Covering Your Scooter

Keeping your scooter clean and dust free keeps it looking newer for a long time. Even if you're storing it indoors for the winter, a cover is a good thing to put on your scoot. Keeping dust off is particularly helpful for the electronic parts that are becoming more common. Dust can also work its way into the paint and can damage the finish over a long period of time. Covering things up protects your finish from UV damage and can also help prevent some scratching if your garage is a high-traffic zone where jacket zippers, grocery bags, or other odds and ends might come into contact with your scooter. If you're meticulous about having a clean scooter, a cover will give you more time for riding and less for cleaning if you use it overnight.

Covering a scooter outside is even more important. Out in the harsh elements your seat, paint, bright work, and rubber all need shelter. The indoor enemies of dust, UV light, and abrasive or scratchy objects are accompanied outdoors by water, bird poop, dirt, and other grime. Covers intended for outdoor use tend to be made of thicker materials; they are relatively waterproof, and have securing straps to prevent the cover from being blown off by high winds.

No matter where you store your scooter, or what you use to cover it, waiting for a little bit to cover it is an important idea. Hot exhaust pipes have been known to melt or otherwise ruin scooter covers. In some rare cases the two items have been known to start fires when combined too soon. These days, exhaust pipes often are even hotter due to the catalytic converters they employ to meet new emissions regulations.

Catalytic exhausts are known to be so hot that they have started wild-fires as some cars have driven over dry grasses. Be cautious about covering your pipe up too soon, and be aware that most objects should not touch the exhaust while it's still warm.

Oil Slick

Putting a cover over a dirty scooter will help grind mud, grime, bugs, or other impurities into the finish. This is especially true if the cover is going to be on for a long time. Before storing a bike for a significant period of time, it really should be washed.

Security

Scooters are among the easiest motor vehicles to steal. Even with the fork locked and the engine digitally immobilized, a few burly bandits can usually just pick up an unsecured scooter and load it into a van or pickup. A truly determined thief will stop at almost nothing to rob you, but there are a number of deterrents that will stop that casual thief and will at least slow down serious ones.

There is an old joke that claims if you're being chased by a shark, you don't have to swim faster than the shark, you just have to swim faster than everyone around you. The same is true when securing your scooter. If yours is more difficult to get, a thief will go for easier pickings.

Kick Start

If your scooter comes standard with an alarm and remote starting system, be sure to use the remote to shut off the engine if you use it to start the engine. Many scooters equipped with these systems do not completely shut down unless the same method used to start the scoot is used to shut it down. Electrical devices will often stay on and will then drain the battery.

When available, a garage or lockable indoor space is the most secure place for a two-wheeled vehicle. Of course, additional precautions need to be taken. Don't leave keys in your scooter. In addition to being as easy as taking candy from a baby, it also can run down your battery. Leaving keys in the garage is also not a particularly bright idea.

Convenient? Absolutely, but it would also be quite convenient for the person robbing you of your beloved scoot. For some, outdoor storage is all that is available, and the following accessories are quite useful.

Alarm Systems

Though standard on some scooters, there is a lot of debate about how effective alarm systems really are. Some owners rely on them for peace of mind and would not live without them. Others claim they do little more than drain batteries. Some of them are not very sensitive, and others are too sensitive, while some can have the sensitivity adjusted. The question then becomes whether your own auditory sensitivity is sufficient to hear the alarm while someone is making off with your vehicular pride and joy. Whether or not people out and about around your scooter are completely desensitized to automotive style alarms is another concern. If nobody seems to care that your scooter's alarm is blaring, how would anybody stop a robber or take enough notice to be a decent witness? Theft can happen so quickly that many recommend using the alarm only to supplement a lock.

In addition to making a lot of loud noise, aftermarket alarms often have extras like pagers and other relay devices that will let you know in real time if your ride is being tampered with. Some have significant range and can alert you even at a serious distance from your scoot. The sensitivity issues still abound. False alarms disrupting your workday would be annoying. Losing your scooter to a gang of very gentle and smooth criminals would be quite a sad and frustrating event. Striking that balance would also be difficult, and real-time remote warning does not address that. It also brings up the possible danger of a confrontation. Many people's initial reaction to the theft of their property would be to go and defend what is rightfully theirs. Those who would break the law to steal might not have many qualms with seriously injuring or possibly even killing the people they are stealing from. It would be tricky to know what to do about someone attempting to make off with your bike.

LoJack systems are also available for motorcycles. In the event that your scooter does get stolen, police can track it down and recover it. Whether or not it will be intact may be another story, but if it is found early enough it may be just fine. Some systems are also known to reduce insurance rates for those who have theft and vandalism coverage.

Cable Locks

Though they can be cut through, cable locks are great for deterring joy riders in low-crime areas. Perhaps not a sufficient deterrent to a professional bandit, they do work well in daylight in high-visibility locations.

Thieves prefer easy prey, and they tend to go for the ones that are the least secured or guarded. The longer they have to work to steal something, the greater their risk of getting caught. If other scooters around yours aren't locked up, even a cable lock can prevent your ride from being purloined.

Cable locks have the primary benefit of being light and compact. Unlike u-locks or heavy chains, they are fairly flexible and usually can be compressed significantly. With extensive lengths of cable available, they can also be used to lash multiple scooters together for security. This is particularly useful at scooter rallies where you cannot securely store your machine in a lockable garage. Using multiple cables on one scoot can also be worthwhile. Hitch up the front wheel, the rear, the leg shield, or find anything else on your scooter that would be secure and difficult to break or unbolt. The more hoops a thief has to jump through, the more he or she will become inclined to look for an easier target.

Scootrivia

Sneaking a motorcycle or scooter into a ground-floor motel room is a very traditional way to try to secure a bike while far away from the safety and comfort of one's own garage. You should still bring a backup form of security to scooter rallies and when you're out doing long-distance touring rides. Most motels and hotels frown upon guests bringing vehicles into the rooms.

U-Locks

Highly recommended on bicycles, they can be good for scooters if they can attach easily to the scooter and to a stationary and secure object. It's more common to see heavy-duty chains used in conjunction with small u-locks. Often referred to as New York chains, they are made of hardened steel. The "New York" name refers to the fact that these are required by many insurers in order to write a policy for theft coverage on one's motorcycle insurance policy in New York City. Serious protection comes at the price of decreased convenience. With a lot more heft and bulk than a cable lock, they can gobble up your storage space pretty easily. In a high-theft area, it can be a small price to pay for peace of mind.

A large u-lock can be used to fasten the rear wheel and shock to something firmly secured. However, the problem with this can often be trying to part and then raise your scooter onto the center stand while keeping it close enough to your intended hitching post. Alternatively, a pair of them could be hooked together if a greater distance needs to be spanned.

Bolt Locks

Appropriately named, the bolt lock provides instant security and additional storage. That's right, security and storage. You gain security by locking up the scooter, and storage by adding a way to lock a helmet or jacket to the scooter. Run a cable through a full-face helmet's mouth guard or the D-rings of other styles or down the sleeve of a jacket, loop on, and lock it up. The only limit is your imagination.

If your scooter has a bolt—you can use it. If you need more than one or need to move the location of the lock and cable(s)—you can add more washers. You simply remove a bolt and add the washer, and screw the bolt back on. You can add thread locker for extra security and to prevent bolts loosening if you wish. It really is that simple.

You don't have to keep the lock attached to the scooter when not in use, so the only visual change to the scooter is the addition of the washer. The lock is small and easily fits into a glove box, underseat compartment, or pocket.

To use the lock, you slide the lock over the washer, run a cable or two through items you want secured, insert the cable end into the lock, and turn the barrel key. That sounds like more than it is. Each lock can secure up to two cables. The cables are available in 12-inch, 18-inch, 6-foot, and 12-foot lengths. The shorter cables can be used to secure helmets and jackets, and the longer cables used for jackets or securing your scooter to other scooters or any other large object.

The steel tubular-cam lock is made in the United States and comes in chrome or powder-coated finishes. The steel-braided cables are vinyl coated to protect from scratching your scooter. While the cables won't stop the most ambitious thief, they will certainly slow him down and hopefully send him on to an easier target.

Other Locks

Some locks are not designed to tie your scooter to a fixed object. Some are intended to impede the use of a scooter.

Grip locks are simple devices that keep the front brake lever and throttle grip from moving. These are usually made of brightly colored, high-impact plastic with steel rods running throughout. Unless you have an extremely heavy scooter, a grip lock is more appropriate as a supplemental deterrent than your primary mode of defense. However, it is an additional hoop to get through, and by virtue of it preventing throttle or brake-lever movement, it makes moving a scooter around significantly harder. Grip locks can also be used on the left grip of the scooter. If you leave your manual-shift scooter in gear, it will also be quite difficult to roll around. The bright coloration tells passersby and thieves alike that you've got an additional security device in your arsenal.

Disc locks attach to the front brake rotor and prevent the front wheel from moving. On a small and light scooter, neither of these items would be particularly effective on their own. Combined with a chain or cable lock, it does make your bike much less attractive prey. On a heavier scooter, these items can be much more effective.

If you don't have a garage or shed to store your scooter in at night, the H-Base lock is a heavy-duty locking system that creates security where there may not be any.

If you're parking in a shed, garage, or on a driveway that isn't secured to your satisfaction, you can now attach your beloved scooter to the concrete. The H-Base doesn't take up much space, but the steel is quite heavy.

Find the location where you'd like to park; this locking system isn't easy to move, so be sure it's the perfect location. If you don't own the concrete where you'd like to park, be sure to get permission to install the H-Base lock.

Using a ½" drill bit, you drill into the concrete, blow out the dust, and add the bolts one at a time to ensure a perfect fit. Be sure to wear eye protection. Once the heavy plate is bolted to the concrete, a slider plate hides the bolts. A heavy chain secures the scooter and a Kryptonite padlock is the final touch that holds it all together.

This is an ingenious way to create a secure parking spot where you need it. A scooter can be locked to it a couple of different ways, but the preferred method is parking directly over the base, and tightening the chain around the floorboard and to the lock. In addition to securing the scooter, it makes it difficult to knock the scooter over or roll it off the center stand, which is quite an added bonus.

Perhaps most importantly, modern scooters, and many vintage scooters, are equipped with fork locks. This keeps the handlebars and the front wheel locked in a left-turn position. It definitely makes a scooter harder to move around and more of a pain for the bandit to deal with if it does get stolen.

Kick Start

If you have theft coverage on your insurance, talk to your agent about locks and theft prevention. She often will have suggestions or requirements you should follow to be covered. She may also be able to offer you discounts for certain optional extras. Even if your agent can't do that, it never hurts to ask.

The Least You Need to Know

◆ Keep your battery warm and charged up.

◆ Add stabilizer, fill the tank, and start the engine for a bit to protect the fuel system during storage.

◆ Give your scooter a bath before putting it to bed.

◆ Covering your scoot keeps it looking shiny and new.

◆ Locks keep honest people honest.

7

Customizing Your Scooter

In This Chapter

- Paint, decals, and vinyl
- Accessories
- Performance upgrades
- Going from mild to wild

Once you get to know your scooter and vice versa, you'll want to add some personal touches to make your statement of style. Whether you choose a modern or retro-style scooter, there are many options to add flair and pizzazz.

External Changes

Cosmetic changes are the most visible way you can trick out your scooter. If you are an extrovert craving attention, there are many alterations you can make to really draw a crowd. Whether in traffic or at a rally showing your scooter, these modifications will surely turn heads.

Kick Start _____

Some custom-paint artists love getting the chance to do scooters because they can do much more than on a motorcycle fuel tank. It's important to find one who knows how to paint on both metal and plastic, because few scooters are entirely steel anymore.

Paint

Though not cheap, a custom paint job can be quite eye catching. Costs depend largely on the complexity of it and what kind of paints you want. On the lower end of the price spectrum you have a one-color re-spray. At the upper end you start seeing multilayered flames executed in shimmering pearl, mica, or metal flake paints.

In either case, the proper way to repaint is to have the scooter almost completely disassembled. This ensures proper coverage and prevents paint being sprayed onto parts that shouldn't be painted. It is also the only sure way to truly change the color of your entire scooter. Removing bodywork and mechanical items really isn't as difficult as it might sound. A mechanically competent owner can do the work to save money. Sandwich bags, permanent markers, and digital photographs are extremely helpful when it comes time to put everything back together.

Don't think that custom paint jobs are only for metal scooters though. Many plastic-bodied scooters have panels that are painted from the factory. If they are made of certain types of ABS plastic, then they are essentially the same as the bumpers on modern cars. With the proper primers and paint additives, these types of plastics can be painted with automotive paints. Some plastics were engineered to be resistant to chemicals, and often tend to resist being painted. There are special primers that work on many of them. The key is to remove panels you would like to paint and look for markings on them that tell the material. Online resources can help decode the markings for you, or take them in to your painter for help.

Scooterists have a long history of doing things themselves, and many have been known to handle their own paint jobs. If you were born with the do-it-yourself gene, then you might get a kick out of spraying your own scooter. While a proper air compressor and paint-gun setup will offer the best results, a lot of practice can yield surprisingly nice results even from spray paint. Some spray paints are formulated for plastics, which would make them useful on some scooters.

Proper surface preparation is the key to every good paint job. A smooth base surface will make the end result smoother. Proper disassembly and masking also make a big difference in the outcome. Anyone who has painted will also tell you to apply several thin coats of paint rather than one or two thick ones to prevent drips and runs in the paint. After the paint dries, it can be sanded with very fine paper, and then more color coats or clear coats can be applied. Buffing can also be done to get that hyper-glossy look.

All told, painting is a process that rewards those who are patient and clever. Do your homework, get the proper respirators, set up a clean and well-ventilated work environment, and you can do a very nice paint job on your own.

David Westman, founder of the Sqream Scooter Club, is the proud owner of the first Atomic Scooter—the "Atomic Blast." It glows in the dark for up to 7 hours after a day in the sun.

(Photo courtesy of David Westman)

If you are planning something more complicated than a simple color change, designing a custom paint scheme up front is another consideration. Paint is more alterable than a tattoo, but it's still expensive and time-consuming to change if you're unhappy with it. Having a clear idea of what you want is only part of the equation. You have to be able to communicate it to your painter. If you're an excellent sketcher, you should work up some drawings. Or take digital pictures and draw what you're wanting on them. If you are not explicit with your painter, you are likely to see a paint job that differs greatly from the one you had in mind. Get things in writing so that if there are mistakes, you have a way to get them resolved.

There is an interesting option for those wanting a custom look on a budget. On many scooters the body panels can be taken off and either repainted or swapped for panels of another color. Several dealers did this with the Genuine Stella. The horn cover and rear cowls were often swapped between two models on the floor. Some dealers also switched out the front fender, though many did not. For example, if a dealer observed that the white and orange models weren't getting much attention, a simple swapping of parts made them much more interesting and appealing. The P series and its offspring from India are very easy to switch over in a short period of time, but the same trick can be applied to many other scooters. Plastic panels are pretty easy to remove, and if you know someone with the same model locally who is willing to trade, you can have a two-tone scooter for nothing more than the time it takes you to remove and replace the bodywork.

Some paint jobs really raise the bar. In the U.K. there are scooters that are rolling canvases for elaborate, photo-realistic, airbrushed paintings. Simple custom work eventually became almost mundane and people turned to building theme bikes to continue to impress the crowds at shows. A brief glance through the British magazines devoted to vintage scooters and that country's scooter scene is inspiring to those who have the fever for customization.

American scooterists are up to the job of giving their counterparts across the pond a run for their money when it comes to theme paint jobs. David Westman's Atomic Blast features ghostly flames that glow in the dark overlaid on metallic greens and yellows that have a positively radioactive glow. The Hot Wheels Lambretta has won trophies and has been featured in magazines, as has the Batman Vespa. Themed bikes are at the opposite end of the custom-paint spectrum from bikes with a change of color or the addition of pin striping.

> **Oil Slick** _____
>
> Modern paints are often toxic; painting is an activity that requires precaution for the sake of one's health and the environment. Always use the recommended safety equipment when painting and work in a properly ventilated area.

Decals and Vinyl

If you're not interested in going for a custom paint job but would like something a little less monochromatic, decals and vinyl are a great way to go. Most cities and large towns have at least one sign shop, if not several, that can cut and apply vinyl graphics to your scooter. Vinyl comes in a rainbow of colors and some of them are even reflective for those who like being seen at night as much as they do during the day. Many sign shops can do design work, or take your designs and cut them for you. Some shops will apply them for you, but some shy away from applying them to vehicles. If you choose to affix the vinyl yourself, you need to do some reading up on how to do it without getting unsightly bubbles. Many shops can also print onto vinyl, which gives you more options for your graphics.

Finding the right sign shop for the job involves knowing what you want up front and being able to communicate it prior to choosing a sign shop to work with.

Decals are another route for those who want splashes of individuality for their scooters. Typically decals are a little flashier than vinyl and have more colors or printed images. Typically decals are not custom-made, but a quick web search will return thousands of results. Decals are perfect if you are open-minded with a general idea of what you want, like flames. They are also great for applying branded items to your scoot, like the logo or image of your favorite childhood toy or cartoon character. As with vinyl, there are application issues to consider. Sticking a decal on a curved surface is a tricky proposition. Bubbles also pop up under decals as they do on vinyl. Of course, all this is with the added complication of an adhesive backing.

Though vinyl and decals are not as permanent as paint, they can be given more permanence with clear coating. This is a clear paint that is typically applied to give colored paints a deeper, glossier finish. If applied over vinyl and decals, it has the same effect while also protecting your artwork. It does make removal of your decals impossible without having to repaint though.

Car wraps are another method of vehicular adornment. They are highly customized and usually include images. They are printed and then applied much like cut vinyl. For those wanting an eye-popping alternative to a custom paint job, wraps certainly deliver. From photo-realistic images to wood grain, anything that can be printed can be turned into a wrap. These are created and applied to vehicles by companies that specialize in wrapping.

Bling Bling

Sparkly jewelry isn't just for celebrities anymore. Your scooter can look like a million bucks with the addition of chrome accessories. Primarily offered for retro-style scooters, there are a number of products that can dress up your ride. Racks, crash bars, and mirrors are all items that will make your scoot glitter like a disco ball. Many of these accessories are reminiscent of those that were found on Mod scooters in the 1960s, which usually had several mirrors and accessory lights.

Chrome can also be plated onto other metal parts of a scooter. Items such as wheels, exhaust pipes, brake levers, and even down to nuts and bolts have all been chromed for custom scoots.

For those who find off-the-shelf accessories to be too common, a custom name badge is just the thing. Badgemaker Deluxe creates chrome badges for scooters and automobiles. From their extensive font library they can design the crowning touch for your personalized scooter. Or they can use your artwork to create that one-of-a-kind piece of bling.

A few people have taken their love for chrome so far as to get their entire scooters plated. It's a very shiny and almost blinding look, but one that is hard to top. As with swapping out body panels, chrome bodywork mixed with painted bodywork makes for a really slick two-tone effect. There are sources for chromed panels for the P series compatible scooters as well as automatic Vespas. Though there are not any off-the-shelf chrome bodywork sources for other plastic body parts, it's possible to have them made. Chromed plastic is more and more common these days, and there are more places than ever to get plastics chromed. So removing your bodywork might be the ticket to getting things shined up. Chrome plating isn't particularly recommended for textured plastics, as the finish won't be as mirror-like as it would be on smooth panels.

A vintage Lambretta with some serious bling.

(Photo by Bev Brinson)

Stella is dressed up and ready to go.

(Photo Courtesy of Genuine Scooters)

Kick Start _____

Buying or borrowing an extra set of wheels to send to the paint shop or powder coater will mean your scooter doesn't have to be out of commission. Within your scooter club or on a brand-specific message board it might be worthwhile to start an exchange program for those who want to add pigment to their rims.

Tires and Wheels

Although functional, tires also have a large impact on the appearance of any vehicle. White-wall tires are a common appearance change made on scooters, particularly to those with retro styling. However, high-grip tires can also dramatically change the look of a scooter with their zigzagging tread patterns, which is a nice side benefit of better performance. Colored tires allow the fashion conscious to color coordinate. For those who need that one-off touch, there are artisans who work exclusively in the gummy medium of tires. These master carvers can take racing slick tires and carve treads into them from your own design. Unless you are already a master tire engineer, it's inadvisable to expect your own design to be comparable to manufactured tires in terms of functionality or safety. On two wheels, custom treads are more for show than anything else.

Chrome rims by MRP add some serious shine.

(Courtesy of Martin Racing Performance)

Aftermarket wheels are not readily available off the shelf for scooters as they are for cars, trucks, and cruiser motorcycles. Even on radically customized scooters, stock wheels are the norm. It would not be impossible for a motivated individual to have a set of custom rims fabricated. However, one need not go to extreme lengths to dress up your rolling stock. Paint and powder coating are easy and relatively inexpensive ways to trick things out.

Nearly all stock alloy and steel wheels for scooters are painted, so they can be painted in other colors without a lot of fuss. As with painting the bodywork, the wheels can be as wild as desired. If your dreams are haunted by visions of a red scooter sporting metallic black wheels with an iridescent pearl coat superimposed, you can get that. If you dream of a blue scooter with simple, ivory-colored wheels, you can get that, too.

The same precautions and advice about painting your own bodywork are common to painting wheels. Prep is extremely important, and in the case of wheels includes removing tires, tubes, and valve stems. Of course, you don't have to stop at just one color. Flames, stripes, airbrushing, and any other paint technique can be done on wheels, and more than likely already has.

Powder coating is similar to paint, but the process is entirely different. Paints are pigments suspended in solvents that evaporate and leave a hardened coating. Powder coating uses electrostatic charges to get plastic powder to the base surface. The powder is then heated and exposed to intense UV light in some cases. The heat melts the plastic, which then hardens as it cools or is cured by the UV exposure.

This process is typically outside the capabilities of the amateur, and is nearly always handled by a powder-coating company. A quick look through the phone book will probably turn up at least one in your area, if not several.

Powder coating comes in several colors and finish options, from matte to glossy. Opaque, translucent, and metallic finishes are also available, just like they would be with paint.

So why use powder coating instead of paint? It has some durability advantages over traditional paints. When the plastic hardens it has more scratch and chip resistance. Drawbacks include a limited choice of colors when compared to paint, and the inability to match powder coating to paint. So it's best for complementing or accenting another color.

Additionally, the resulting coating tends to be a bit thicker than paint. While fine in many applications, it can be a problem where clearances are already tight, or where small details might be obscured. In applications where a deep-looking glossy finish is desired, paint tends to look richer and more sophisticated. Most scooters will never be customized to a level where that matters, so powder coating is highly recommended for an attractive and highly durable custom touch for your scooter.

The chrome fetish can also be extended to one's rims. Tires and valve stems must be removed, and the wheels will need to be stripped of all paint. A good chrome shop should be capable of doing the prep work for you. If you have lug bolts or nuts, don't forget to get them chromed to match.

Accessory Lighting

In the 1960s the Mods not only bedazzled their scoots with mirrors and bits of chrome, they also added lights galore. It would not have been all that surprising to see a Vespa or Lambretta with a dozen or more lights on the leg shield in the right parts of London. These days, those with nostalgia for those days are attaching lights to their retro-styled scooters. Some of the accessory lights for the vintage scoots fit the modern manual scooters. A little alteration to fit hasn't stopped owners of retro automatic scooters, though.

Over the years tastes have changed, and colored lighting has become popular on cars and motorcycles and is now making its way onto scooters. Universal kits for neon lighting are finding their way under the floorboards of many types of scooter. Flexible strips of LEDs can provide the same effect that neon does, but can be packed into much smaller places. LED replacements for conventional brake and turn-signal bulbs have also become popular. They are often brighter than stock bulbs and use less electricity.

Internal Modifications

Barring louder exhaust pipes, performance modifications generally are not blatantly obvious. Though not as overt as cosmetic changes, they offer scooter owners another way to personalize their bikes, and have a fan base among those who love to tinker with machines. Many of the

following parts are available on two- and four-stroke engines, but tend
to have more impact on two-strokes.

Exhaust Pipes

Four-stroke scooters usually see only modest performance gains from
aftermarket exhaust systems. When used in combination with other
tuning parts, the performance improvements are more noticeable. More
easily perceptible is the increase in volume. Nearly all aftermarket pipes
are louder than stock, and many have exhaust notes that are music to
the ears of some scooterists. Typically, they aren't as loud as open pipes
on V-twin cruisers, but it would not be impossible to run afoul of the
law or annoy the neighbors.

*A custom Leo Vince pipe will
have your scooter singing a
throaty song.*

*(Photo Courtesy of LeoVince
Exhaust Systems)*

A properly tuned expansion chamber pipe will offer clear increases in
performance on a two-stroke engine. Pipe design or selection is a bit of
a dark art, so it pays to do the research and to choose the right pipe to
use with any other modifications you have made or plan to make. Find
people who have tuned up their scooters. Replicate the setup that will
best meet your goals. If you already have an engine kit and a larger carburetor, you need a different pipe than someone who has not made any
other modifications.

For those who aren't looking for an increase in performance or noise,
there are a few ways to change the look for a stock pipe. Most stock
exhausts are made of mild steel and painted with high-temperature
paints. Steel readily lends itself to being chromed, and a few people
have had their pipes stripped of paint and given a fancy coat of bling.
Removal of the heat shield and mounting tabs for a cleaner look is also
quite common prior to plating.

> **Kick Start**
>
> If you are considering a pipe, try to find an audio file of one on a scooter like yours. It will give you an idea of what kind of sound to expect. It might also give you an inkling of how loud it is. Pipes are usually not returnable after being fitted. A little research can prevent an expensive mistake.

Cylinder Kits

An inconspicuous start to building a *sleeper*, big cylinder kits increase the power output of an engine. The power increase comes from an increase in displacement. 50cc engines typically jump up to 70cc. Four-stroke engines also have cylinder kits to increase displacement. Performance camshafts are available for some four-strokes, and if you plan to use one in conjunction with a cylinder kit, it is cheaper to install both at the same time. Though prices for the kits themselves are quite reasonable, the labor to install them can be as much as the kit itself, if not more. Factor that into your tuning budget if you can't do the labor yourself.

Some kits are made of cast iron while others are aluminum. Nikasil-coated liners are another option on some kits. There are a number of choices, each with advantages and potential drawbacks. Picking the right one depends largely on performance goals. Some kits make massive amounts of power, but have very little longevity. They are intended for on-track racing use only, and the power bands are rarely ideal for street use. Street-use kits tend to last longer at the expense of power output. However, the power they do make is usually available without having to rev the engine to stratospheric rpms.

def•i•ni•tion

A **sleeper** is a vehicle that appears to be unmodified with hidden performance enhancements. Typically underestimated, they are known to surprise unsuspecting victims at stoplights.

In addition to adding the kit, the carburetor will probably need to be rejetted, especially on a two-stroke engine. Getting everything dialed in just right is a really important part of the tuning process. Again, if you cannot do it yourself, then you need to have someone with experience fine-tune all of your settings for you.

Carburetor

When changes are made to the engine, the amount of fuel and air needed to optimize performance changes. Changing carb jets is a common practice with many parts like pipes or cylinder kits. On two-strokes, upgrading to a larger carburetor is also common among those looking for larger performance increases. Not all carburetors are the same. Most scooters come with CV, or constant velocity, carburetors. In some cases, people looking to move up the performance ladder will switch over to flat slide carburetors, which have the advantage of allowing more air to flow in full-throttle and high-rpm situations.

Additional performance can come in the form of an altered air filter for some scooters, by allowing more air to flow into the carburetor and more fuel to mix with it before reaching the engine. Not all carburetors will tolerate air-box changes. The most common issue is that the air and fuel mixture will go too lean (too much air and not enough fuel).

Running too lean can cause overheating, knocking, and detonation. These issues can lead to your engine seizing up, or even burning through vital engine components. When a carb is set up to run too rich (too much fuel for the amount of air coming in), there are other problems. The spark plug can be fouled pretty easily. Heavy deposits of carbon can build up in the engine and the exhaust. Running too lean or rich can cause drivability problems like bogging down or poor throttle response. Properly setting up a carburetor for a performance engine takes experience and is not a task for unsupervised novices.

Oil Slick

Changing carburetors may require other changes to your scooter. Most automatic scooters have automatic choke systems for starting and initial idling. Most performance carburetors have manual chokes, which will require fitting a choke pull or lever somewhere. Performance carburetors typically do not have oil-injection systems. On a two-stroke this means you will have to premix your fuel and oil.

Computers and CDIs

As fuel-injected scooters come onto the market, performance-equipment manufacturers are expanding into the chip-tuning market that is huge for modern cars. With changes to the engine-management software there are often performance increases to be had. Direct-injected scooters like the Aprilia SR50 Ditech are at the forefront of computer tuning for scooters. The direct-injection system can be diagnosed and tuned, and the ignition timing and fuel injection can be remapped with various data files that are available. Vespa's GTS250ie is also fuel injected, and companies like Malossi are working on reprogrammed chips to improve performance.

def•i•ni•tion

The **Capacitive Discharge Ignition (CDI)** is common in the majority of new scooters. It is an electronic system that fires the spark plug to ignite fuel and air in the engine.

Scootrivia

Aprilia's SR50 Ditech and other scooters with the direct-injection system from Orbital use a Nintendo GameBoy for engine diagnostics and reprogramming.

On carbureted scooters there is often room for improvement to the *Capacitive Discharge Ignition (CDI)*. Many CDI boxes have built-in rev limiters that restrict the performance of the engine. Connecting a wire differently or clipping it completely can disable some CDI rev limiters. This is especially true on 50cc two-stroke scooters. Before whipping out the cutting pliers, get good advice from someone who has actually done the job on which wire to cut or otherwise connect. Aftermarket CDI systems can offer performance increases by eliminating the rev limiter or by altering the ignition timing.

Transmission

One of the major advantages of a CVT is the tuning potential it has. As you change engine parts for more power, the ratios and transmission response will also need to change. There are a lot of easily replaceable parts that can help make use of your engine's new characteristics. Changing the weight of your roller weights can alter the top speed or acceleration of your machine. A variator kit will give you different ramps for the roller weights and tends to improve your acceleration and top-speed characteristics. A broad range of differing weights of rollers are available to fit variator kits, which allows more fine tuning.

The clutch springs can also be replaced with performance springs to change when the clutch engages. Aftermarket clutches with different friction compounds are also available to withstand augmented power and torque, or to engage more quickly. The torque spring controls your rear pulley. It has an impact on the acceleration and top-speed characteristics of a CVT. Changing out the torque spring can help you achieve your performance goals when combined with the proper modifications. Kevlar-reinforced belts don't actually improve performance much but have a longer life and are meant to withstand the increased power of a tuned engine.

Up-gear kits are also available to change the final gearing to the rear axle. These usually sacrifice a bit of acceleration for more top speed and should only be used on highly tuned engines.

Manual-shift scooters also have transmission modifications that can be made, but they are typically more expensive and labor intensive than those for automatics. For the Stella and P-series engines, the option exists to convert to a five-speed transmission. Alternatively, with the many incarnations and variations of the P-series engine, there are a number of different gear ratios offered by the factory over the years. Many of them can be interchanged or mixed and matched to suit.

Unlike variator tuning, this is not an easy job. It involves removing the engine and transmission from the scooter, and then disassembling many major components and reversing the procedure to put it all back together. Changing the parts may be difficult, but selecting them can also be complex. Knowing what gear ratios are appropriate for your power band requires expertise. This is a task suited for seasoned tuners. If you have one you can hire, it's well worth it, because the alternative is a scooter that does not perform as well after the changes.

Nitrous Oxide Kits

The darling of the import tuner car scene, nitrous-oxide kits (or nitrous) have trickled down to scooters. On automatic scooters they are intended more for brief top-speed gains or to maintain a speed uphill instead of providing brutal acceleration. On manual-shift scooters they are more like on a car, but

> **Oil Slick**
> Nitrous is known to blow up engines when used improperly. Proper setup by an expert is vital.

caution still should be exercised. The systems are very expensive, and if used improperly they can destroy an engine. Simply put, nitrous is not for everyone.

The Least You Need to Know

◆ Paint is cool, but vinyl and decals offer some of the look without the price.

◆ Chrome may not get you home, but it will get you noticed.

◆ Performance upgrades keep you from being all show and no go.

◆ Your imagination and wallet are the only limits to how radically custom you can go.

Part 3

Fun Stuff

Once your scooter is all dressed up, it's time to get some gear to adorn yourself—helmets, eyewear, jackets, boots, raingear, and more. It's a good idea to buy equipment you can wear for years to come. While stylish, this gear is also your last defense against road rash and other potential injuries.

There are backpacks and courier bags in every shape and size to fit your needs, and storage options galore so you can take it all (almost) with you. We'll also discuss clubs, rallies, and cross-country rides—there are many events to particpate in. Or be the rebel and go it alone!

Chapter 8

Protective Clothing

In This Chapter

- Protecting head, shoulders, knees, toes
- Eyewear
- Comfort vs. safety
- Extreme gear

Now that your scooter is all tricked out, it's time to accessorize yourself. People on two wheels tend to migrate toward black as the choice in riding wear—but keep visibility in mind. There are many colorful choices in all accessories. Should you unexpectedly leave your scooter at speed, you can minimize damage by maximizing your protection.

Buying riding gear is also an intensely personal process. Some people feel naked without being dressed from head to toe in full-out racing leathers; others take a much more casual approach. This chapter covers a broad spectrum of gear to show that there is something out there for everyone.

Helmets

It is important to look for DOT or Snell stickers on helmets to know what standards a helmet conforms to. DOT approval is required in states that have helmet laws. The Snell Memorial Foundation sets voluntary standards for helmets, which are tougher than DOT. Snell approval denotes the highest level of head protection you can buy in America. Snell tests and certifies helmets that meet or exceed the performance requirements they have set forth. The DOT approves helmets on an honor system but does do some spot testing to ensure compliance. Essentially the manufacturer is supposed to test the helmet, and if it meets DOT standards, then they are allowed to say it is DOT approved.

Though DOT approval and Snell certification are the standards to look for, there are helmets on the market that do not meet either. In a state where helmets are required, they do not qualify as legitimate helmets. They are also not recommended because they do not appear to be designed to meet any specific performance criteria.

Ventilation is an important attribute to look for on a helmet, particularly on a full-face or flip-up. Keeping a cool head just makes riding much more pleasant. Replaceable foam padding inside your helmet also is a nice feature to look for. Some of that padding can be washed or otherwise cleaned if removed from the hard shell. Being able to get the funk out of your helmet after a long ride on a hot day is worthwhile.

Nearly all helmets can be upgraded for visibility with the addition of reflective tape or vinyl. In Chapter 7 we discussed getting vinyl graphics cut. The same process works for your helmet as well. Extremely reflective tapes are also available to play the same role. Some are even available as sheets of material. A little fiddling with an exacto knife and you can create almost any custom shape or design your mind can dream up and your hands can execute.

Visors and face shields are options for many helmets, particularly on half- and open-face helmets. Almost any helmet with a shield will usually have visor or shield-replacement options. Typically there will be shields that are tinted, anti-fogging, polarized, or just plain clear. The options you have depend largely on the manufacturer of your helmet.

Another benefit of this is that if your face shield gets scratched up a bit over time, you can replace it. Getting pummeled by suicidal insects and the little sand and gravel pieces that get kicked up by cars and trucks can really do in a face shield in a surprisingly short amount of time. Better to replace a shield that costs $10 to $20 once in a while than to get hit in the face.

> **Kick Start** _____
>
> When shopping for a helmet, try several on. The safest helmet is the one you will actually wear; comfort is paramount. An uncomfortable helmet can also cause fatigue. If a helmet seems to fit well initially, keep it on for about 15 minutes to see how it fares. Each helmet and each head has its own unique shape. It takes some time to see if a helmet actually fits your head.

Skull Cap (Half-Helmet)

Also known as a half-helmet, this type of brain bucket covers the upper part of a rider's head. The ears, face and much of the head are not covered. Though better than nothing, this helmet is the least protective. Some riders do like them because they feel they have better peripheral vision and because they feel they can hear more.

Three-Quarter (Open-Face) Helmet

With protection for the base of the skull and over the ears, a three-quarter, or open-face, helmet offers more protection than a half-helmet. They are often available with detachable or pivoting face shields that are helpful in deflecting bugs, gravel, and other objects that might otherwise make painful contact with your face. Some riders prefer these helmets because of the added protection they offer while leaving the face area open. Often wearers of this type of helmet claim to feel less claustrophobic in an open-face than they do in a full-face helmet.

Full-Face Helmet

The top of the line in head protection, the full-face picks up where the open-face helmet leaves off. In addition to covering the whole head, a full-face has a chin bar and pivoting visor to protect the rider's entire face. A growing body of evidence suggests that a large number of head impacts occur in the chin area. As such, this is generally our recommendation when people ask what helmet to get. Although initially many riders complain of feeling a bit trapped and closed in, many riders later describe feeling naked in anything less than a full-face helmet.

This full-face Shoei Helmet has different colored shields available, which can be changed easily for different lighting conditions.

(Photo by Bev Brinson)

Flip-Up Helmet

For the convenience of an open-face and the safety of a full-face, a flip-up (also called ratchet-jaw) helmet is a nice compromise. Flip-ups are not yet Snell tested or certified because Snell has not yet figured out a way to test the release mechanisms. However, there are a number of DOT-approved flip-ups, many of which come from helmet families that do have Snell certifications. While most are not intended to be open while riding, they are nice when filling up your tank, putting on glasses or sunglasses, or simply attempting to talk with someone. Many riders who feel uncomfortable in conventional full-face helmets find that they are comfortable in flip-ups. The ability to open the chin bar and keep things open at stoplights or when not moving is highly appealing

A vintage Lambretta with custom horns and tail pipe.

(Photo by Bev Brinson)

Themed scooters are popular in Europe. This vintage Batman-themed scooter was Photographed at the Mile High Mayhem rally.

(Photo by Bev Brinson)

This red Stella is fully dressed in chrome.

(Photo courtesy of Genuine Scooters)

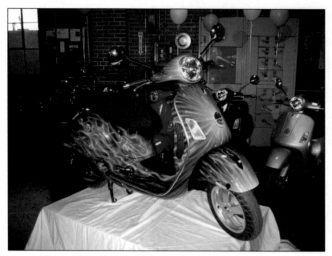

By day the Atomic Blast has subtle flames; by night its glow in the dark paint grabs and reflects all light.

(Photo courtesy of David Westman)

The Genuine Black Cat 50cc scooter features Black Cat fire cracker graphics.

(Photo courtesy of Genuine Scooters)

The Honda Metropolitan is available in a variety of patterns and has a lower seat height than most.

(Photo courtesy of American Honda Motor Co. Inc.)

Scooters can do good! A portion of the proceeds from the HOPE model from Schwinn supports breast cancer awareness and research.

(Photo courtesy of Schwinn)

The Eton Beamer is a sporty 50cc scooter.

(Photo courtesy of Eton)

The Kymco People S 50 is an updated version of one of the most popular 50cc scooters.

(Photo courtesy of STR Motorsports)

The TGB R50X 49cc scooter offers sporty styling and a comfortable ride.

(Photo courtesy of Cobra Powersports)

Introduced in spring of 2006, the Buddy has quickly become one of the most popular scooters. The Genuine Buddy is available as a 50cc or 125cc.

(Photo courtesy of Genuine Scooters)

The Honda Big Ruckus sports the rugged "naked bike" look. The seat folds up to create a backrest when there is no passenger.

(Photo courtesy of American Honda Motor Co. Inc.)

The Vespa GTS 250 features all-metal body panels and is the most powerful Vespa to date.

(Photo courtesy of Vespa USA)

The Piaggio BV 250 is a mid-size upright scooter.

(Photo courtesy of Piaggio USA)

The Honda Reflex has a reclined riding position.

(Photo courtesy of American Honda Motor Co. Inc.)

The Suzuki Burgman 400 is newly designed for 2007.

(Photo courtesy of American Suzuki Motor Corp.)

Kymco introduced the Xciting 500 in 2006.

(Photo courtesy of STR Motorsports)

The Honda Silver Wing has a 582cc liquid-cooled four-stroke parallel-twin engine that can easily be ridden cross-country.

(Photo courtesy of American Honda Motor Co. Inc.)

The Aprilia Scarabeo 500 is a maxi-scooter that offers an upright position for riders.

(Photo courtesy of Vespa USA)

Trikes will soon be available through Colorado Scooters. With a combination of hand and foot brakes, these trikes offer riders flexibility.

(Photo courtesy of Colorado Scooters)

The TGB Delivery scooter can hold pizza and much more!

(Photo courtesy of Cobra Power Sports)

The Diamo Velux is a conve ible scooter with a retractabl top that is available in 150c and 200cc.

(Photo courtesy of LS Motorspor

The Suntrike from Modcycle has two wheels up front. It's a fun, unique way to scoot around town.

(Photo courtesy of Modcycles)

The Bajaj Auto rickshaw is a three-wheeled convertible scooter.

(Photo courtesy of Bajaj/Argo USA)

to people who want a higher level of safety but don't like feeling as confined as they do in a conventional full-face.

Electronics for Your Helmet

Integrated and add-on electronics are a recent trend in helmets. Some helmets can be purchased with Bluetooth headsets already incorporated. Most helmets can be retrofitted with kits available from several manufacturers. With a Bluetooth-capable phone you can use your cell phone while riding. Many cell phones really see a drop in battery life when using Bluetooth, but if your scooter came equipped with a 12-volt socket, you are ready to rock and roll. Some audio players are also supported, which would enable you to have music as you ride.

> **Oil Slick**
>
> Some researchers claim that using the phone while driving or riding is inherently a very dangerous activity, even if using a hands-free device. Listening to music while riding is another activity many consider distracting. Being unable to hear ambient noises over music or phone calls is also considered risky.

Heads-up displays are also available for some full-face helmets. When the hardware is installed on your bike and on your helmet, you get projections on your face shield displaying your present speed, engine rpm, and the gear you are in, if applicable.

Eyewear

Though many states don't require helmets, most require some sort of eye protection be worn while riding, and rightly so. You need your eyes to be in tip-top shape to ride, and having them water because of wind does not help that. Rocks, sand, bugs, and other debris also do not belong in them. If you have a full-face helmet, or an open-face with a shield, then you're covered. If you don't have a shield, then you should look into protective eyewear.

Kick Start _____

Layering polarized lenses is a bad idea. If your face shield is polarized or if your windscreen is, it's inadvisable to wear polarized sunglasses. It causes odd color patterns and can obscure details of the road around you. The effects are often significantly amplified at sunrise or sunset.

Glasses

In some states, safety glasses and sunglasses are considered acceptable eye protection. Other states require DOT approval. There are a number of companies that specialize in motorcycle-specific glasses. A number of tints are available. Conventional, dark sunglass lenses are common. Amber and yellow lenses that reduce glare during both night and day are also quite popular. Clear lenses exist for night riding and use on days that aren't sunny or bright.

Goggles

For those who get dry eyes easily, goggles can be a great solution. Most riding goggles have ventilation and are designed not to fog up, but because they are not as open as normal glasses, many wearers say they don't notice their eyes being so dried out. Goggles do a better job covering the entire eye and sealing out fine debris particles like sand and dust. Commonly offered with the same tints and lenses as riding-specific glasses are, there are many that are DOT compliant.

Scootrivia

Goggles are also available for dogs that have the good fortune of riding in sidecars attached to scooters.

Options for Eyeglass Wearers

For those with prescription eyewear, some goggles are designed to go over glasses comfortably. As with regular goggles, many of them are intended to conform to DOT regulations.

This kit from Garny has an option for prescription lenses, converts from glasses to goggles, and has different-colored lenses. It's a very flexible kit whether you wear glasses or not.

(Photo by Bev Brinson)

Jackets

A good riding jacket is one of the best places to start in your quest for protective gear. Selecting a jacket requires you to identify the conditions you'll mostly be wearing it in, as well as your personal safety goals. You will probably discover that you need more than one jacket if you ride in a variety of temperatures. Very few jackets can do it all. A mesh jacket would probably not be very comfortable later in autumn or early in spring, and it might be downright cold if worn in the winter. A great winter riding jacket would be far too hot most of the year. If you are planning to ride year around, or close to it, figuring out a comprehensive package of jackets and gear becomes your task.

Armored Jacket

If you find breaking bones or major bruises to be a hassle, then you're a good candidate for an armored jacket. There are several types of armor ranging from flat, foam pads all the way to molded, dual-density pieces with European Certification. Beyond that, the foams can also be attached to hard plastic or carbon fiber shells to further soften an impact. *CE armor* tends to be more expensive, but it's got excellent protective characteristics. In many jackets it's included as standard, while in others it's optional. Finally, armor is also available that simply straps on.

Flat padding is better than nothing, but it is not usually particularly ideal. Any of the levels of CE armor will offer you good impact protection, with level three offering the most. Whether integrated into riding gear, or strapped on separately, only you can make the decision between comfort and the ultimate level of safety you feel necessary. Talking to other scooterists and motorcycle riders can give you somewhat of a feel for what your peers are wearing and why, but at the same time don't let anyone pressure you into wearing something you're not comfortable with. If you are not comfortable with the gear you purchased, then you are less likely to actually wear it, or wear it habitually.

def•i•ni•tion

Three levels of certification are offered for armor sold on the European market. Level three is the most protective, and is required in racing. Level one is for slower riding and can absorb half the impact of level three. A **CE** label means a product is certified to meet all applicable laws and guidelines in the European Union.

Abrasion-Resistant Materials

Abrasion resistance is another important factor to consider. Armor may protect you from the forces of impact, but it won't stop you from getting scraped up. A material that won't rip, wear through, or melt is what you will need.

Leather is still the gold standard in terms of resisting abrasion. As such, it is the default material for protection in nearly all types of motorcycle racing. Until some of the recent performance textiles, leather was the standard material of most protective gear. It covered riders who wanted to slide knees on sport bikes all the way to those with a more outlaw image on cruisers.

Within the past several years many textiles have entered the protective-gear market that work quite well on the street and offer some benefits that leather cannot. There is no substitute for doing your homework, as some mesh materials have low melting temperatures. If not reinforced in key areas, they will not necessarily provide the protection you desire. Many of the big names in gear have tested their products and can be trusted. Materials like Cordura, ballistic nylon, and aramids such as Kevlar are being used in more and more products that offer new concepts of protection and provide improvements over leather in the areas of ventilation, water protection, and in some cases even abrasion resistance.

When shopping you may see some textiles referred to as having a certain denier number. That number refers to the fiber mass of the cloth. A higher number indicates, in this case, a sturdier fabric. When shopping it's important to really look for good materials and robust construction.

Ventilation

Heat is a key element of rider fatigue. Riding in hot weather just wears you out quickly. Fortunately many gear manufacturers have added vents to jackets, and others have made entire jackets out of mesh. The choice you make depends largely on your local temperatures. In high heat and humidity, a mesh jacket might be more comfortable. In a place with warmer temps during the day and cooler temps at night, a jacket with vents that open and close might be the answer. Other jackets have zip-out liners that enable you to use one jacket over a broader range of temperatures.

No matter what you buy, be sure that it will breathe the way you need it to for the conditions you plan to ride in. Staying comfortable while riding is one of the most overlooked safety procedures of riding.

Airbag Options

As an additional level of protection, there are inflatable vests and jackets that can protect you if you leave your scooter unexpectedly. A lanyard attaches to your scooter and to the jacket. When a certain amount of force is applied, it separates from the jacket and opens a valve that allows carbon dioxide to rapidly inflate pouches in the jacket or vest.

Scootrivia

Wearable airbags have been around for several years, but now some motorcycle and scooter manufacturers are unveiling concept bikes that have airbags actually built in. Presently the Honda Goldwing Airbag is the only model available in the United States. It is one interesting way among many that manufacturers are conceptually addressing safety concerns.

It's very important to remember to unhook the lanyard from your scooter when you park it. Airbag vests and jackets inflate very abruptly and have been known to cause bruising to some people. Minor bruises are quite preferable to more major injuries, to be sure. After forgetting to unfasten the lanyard and getting a few bruises, most riders learn quickly to unhook it and don't make that mistake more than once.

The Airetronics Airbag vest provides added protection, should you unexpectedly leave your scooter.

(Photo by Bev Brinson)

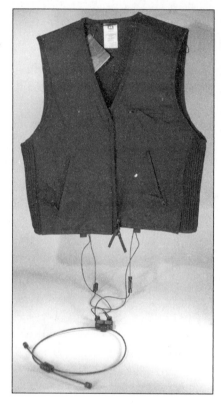

Pants

Many riders often forget that their legs need protection, just like their torsos. Accidents are unpredictable and there is no way of guessing even in the moment which part of the body will hit first and which parts will slide. Stepping up to being protected all around is the safest bet to make.

Are Jeans Enough?

They are better than nothing, but they aren't able to hold up to long slides on the pavement. They do work to some degree in very slow-speed crashes. However, they don't have the abrasion-resistance properties of specially designed riding pants. Denim also has been known to transfer some friction to skin beneath it. While jeans might prevent a serious scrape, they will still often remove a layer or two of skin. Though there are jeans available with aramid fibers for improved anti-abrasion properties, they are not armored and have not yet been shown to be as protective as other types of riding pants.

Armored Pants

Just as with your upper body, armor can help protect your knees. Since knees are useful for walking and rather necessary to riding, they might be worth protecting. CE armor is available for knees. Some armor only covers the kneecaps; other types are more like the shin guards worn by soccer players. Lower-body armor is available in as many flavors as upper-body armor and can be purchased integrated into overpants or separately to strap on.

Several types of textile and leather overpants are available. Some are quite similar to normal pants, except for their material composition and provisions for armor. Others have long zippers running up the outside of the leg. Unzip the sides of the pants and they are much easier to put on, particularly when wearing boots and jeans. This is another place not to let people overly influence your decision. While racing leather pants may offer the ultimate protection, will you actually go through the process of putting them on before riding to work, and will you reverse the process when you get there? Protective gear can only keep you safe if you actually wear it.

Leathers and Chaps

Many jackets have corresponding pants you can buy, but some riders prefer a single-garment suit. Traditionally these have been made of leather and have been used by motorcycle racers or those who desperately wanted to look like racers. As textiles have invaded the market, single-piece textile suits have also come into fashion. They often appear geared toward long-distance touring riders. Typically they offer good ventilation or excellent weather protection. Such suits may not be the most common choice for scooter riders, particularly commuters, but they are out there for riders who prefer the single-piece design.

Chaps are another option that many motorcyclists have used for years. If made of heavier-weight leather, they do offer much of the anti-abrasion properties of leather riding pants. This is also contingent on a fastening system that won't be ripped open easily. Unlike other leg-protection products already discussed, chaps are rarely armored. CE armor can be strapped on underneath for those who like the look and feel of wearing chaps.

Gloves

When you fall, the natural tendency is to put your arms out to catch yourself. It's an instinctive response that doesn't disappear when you get on a two-wheeler. You never realize how many things your palms touch everyday until they are scraped up. A simple pair of gloves can do a lot to protect one of the most vulnerable parts of your body.

For Summer

There are a number of gloves that will protect your hands without warming them up. Many have vents, perforations, or even mesh in between the fingers. Good palm and knuckle protection is what you want to look for.

Summer gloves run the gamut from simple leather ones to gloves made of carbon fiber, leather, and metal mesh with gauntlets running up well beyond the wrist. Textiles have entered the world of hand protection as they have all other forms of protective gear. Textile gloves have an advantage when it comes to being breathable.

As with the rest of your gear, the level of protection or comfort you choose is entirely up to you. If an inexpensive pair of deerskin gloves makes you feel comfortable, then enjoy them. If you cannot stomach the thought of wiping out without Kevlar-reinforced gloves with carbon-fiber knuckle protectors, then that's the route you need to go.

For Winter

When you do need to keep warm, special winter gloves are available to protect your hands in a crash and from the wind chill when riding at speed. Some are even available with heating elements that can be wired to the bike. Others are meant to work in combination with heated grips. Often they use materials like Gore-Tex or 3M Thinsulate to keep your fingers wiggling and frostbite free.

Warm hands are extremely important. Cold hands often do not have the flexibility or strength to operate brake or clutch levers. Obviously that can be a serious problem when it comes time to stop. Thoroughly insulated gloves can also be a good place to put hand warmer packs on particularly cold days. Be careful to get the ones that are meant for in-glove use. Some are too hot for it. As with all things, read the labels first.

Handlebar Muffs

For those who are really serious about cold-weather riding, handlebar muffs really keep the wind off your hands and create a little pocket of air that stays warm. They are insulated and the shell is nearly always a wind-breaking fabric. Originally intended for snowmobiles, they are also used on ATVs and can be strapped onto scooters with relative ease. In combination with heated grips, many riders have said they can ride without even needing gloves for temperature, allowing thinner and more flexible summer gloves to be used year round.

Oil Slick

Handlebar muffs may be easy to strap on, but heated grips are a trickier item. Be sure that your scooter is up to the task of powering them before adding them. Additionally, find grips to replace yours before removing them.

Boots

Footwear is commonly overlooked in protective gear. As with every other part of the body, covering up is the best way to prevent and minimize injuries. An abundance of options in safe footwear for riding makes it hard to go very far wrong.

These Sidi riding boots are not only stylish but also have steel supports over the ankle for protection.

(Photo by Bev Brinson)

Boot Styles

Unlike some of the other riding attire, boots and shoes don't necessarily need to be motorcycle-specific. While there are many types of specialized boots, regular ones with thick soles and leather will also work. An optimal pair of boots will come up over the ankle and are made of durable materials. A sole with some grip is also useful, so cowboy boots are not the best choice.

Scootrivia
If you are interested in a certain subculture look, many of the boots worn by various groups are generally considered to be protective. Combat boots, Doc Martens, and other types of boots that have had some popularity with scooterists over the years aren't just worn for their aesthetic appeal.

Riding-specific boots tend to be made of leather or textiles. Some have an old-school look and are definitely intended to appeal to the cruiser bike crowd. Others match those sets of racing leathers discussed earlier in this chapter in the "Leathers and Chaps" section. Finally, there are some that are intended to work well with textile riding gear. These tend to have better ventilation than normal leather boots. Also, they are usually pretty easy to put on and take off quickly—an asset if you're wearing them to the office and want to change shoes when you get there.

Added Protection

There is debate back and forth as to whether steel-toe boots are really safe to wear when riding. Research suggests that some of the horror stories about losing one or several toes while wearing reinforced boots in an accident would yield the same result or worse without steel toes. Many motorcycle boots do have hard protective pieces in the toes and ankles for extra protection. Again, it comes down to the balance between protection and comfort that each individual has to make. The consensus seems to be that the bare-minimum requirement to consider one's feet protected is that you're wearing sturdy boots that come up over the ankle.

Rainwear

Though many won't ever ride in the rain, some riders just cannot live without riding. Rain gear was created for their comfort. Typically it consists of water-shedding attire to put over your normal gear. Rain gear essentially works by covering you in water-shedding fabrics that are sealed at the seams. Elastics are used at various points to keep water out. If worn properly, it can keep you quite dry even in hard rains.

Generally, it does not contain armor, is not abrasion resistant, and is not intended to defend you from injury. So it's a good idea to wear it over your favorite protective gear when you have less grip and traction and more risk of an accident.

The Least You Need to Know

◆ A full-face helmet is the best head protection.

◆ Listen to your mom: wear a jacket. This time it will protect you from injury instead of catching a cold.

◆ Gloves should be worn as often as your helmet.

◆ Riding pants can literally save your backside.

◆ While there are many types of specialized boots for riding, regular ones with thick soles and leather will also work.

◆ Rain and winter gear expands your riding opportunities.

Chapter 9

Accessories

In This Chapter

- Increasing your cargo capacity
- Additional wind protection
- Bags for riding
- Aftermarket electronics

From additional storage to the latest gadgets, you can add as many or as few options as you prefer. These options are less about looking pretty than making the absolute most of an already practical form of transportation. Most of these accessories are for those who subscribe to the philosophy that chrome won't get the groceries home. Some of the products mentioned are specifically intended for scooters or motorcycles. Others are things that just naturally lend themselves to riding or are very easily adapted. When riding becomes your way of life, you tend to look at any store you see as a potential scooter-accessory shop.

Top Boxes

The top box or case features lockable, and usually watertight, storage. With most manufacturers offering optional top boxes for most models, it is the most common new scooter accessory. Your dealer can set you up with a case that should match your scooter's paint, and backrest upholstery that matches your seat. Typically these bolt onto whatever rear rack or grab-rail setup your scooter has, though a few have different mounting systems that your dealer will install.

Givi makes a wide range of cases to add storage to your bike.

(Photo by Bev Brinson)

The factory isn't the only place to get a top case. Some aftermarket manufacturers make standardized ones that will fit many different makes and models. Though they generally are not color matched to the scooter, they often have more storage space or more useful shapes than some of the factory options. The other benefit is that many of them have provisions to wire up lights so you have extra brake lights for better visibility. Since top cases obscure the standard brake light on some scooters, this can be a critical feature.

Givi also makes top cases with a locking mount that allows them to be detached. The Monolock system has one key for opening the case and detaching it from the scooter. When traveling, it makes your journey a little easier by enabling you to simply take your luggage in to your hotel room. It can also be fairly useful for your office stuff, and gives you a quick and easy way to carry your valuable stuff inside so it doesn't get left out with your scooter where it might be vulnerable.

When purchasing a top case, consider its quality. If the one offered by the factory seems flimsy, then consider going to an aftermarket one. If you are going to use your top case for lockable storage while you're away from the bike, something that looks and feels secure is preferable.

Size is another reason to go after-market. You do get more options and different shapes. So if a factory top case cannot hold a full-face helmet, or two of them, then an aftermarket one would be the way to go. Some after-market cases can also be painted to match your scooter if you can't stand things not matching.

Scootrivia
Many top cases are padded at the front so they can double as a passenger backrest.

Side Storage

When there just isn't sufficient storage under the seat, and when top cases can't even do enough (or are aesthetically offensive), side storage is an option.

Hard Side Cases

Some maxi-scooters have factory-optional side cases, but very few smaller scooters do. As with top boxes, there are aftermarket side cases. Givi makes a series of Monokey side cases that attach and detach in the same manner as the Monolock top cases. This works quite nicely for carrying your stuff to the office or out on longer trips. However, mounting any side cases can be a little tricky. There are some fittings for a few models, but typically, you are on your own figuring out the mounting system. If your scooter doesn't have a specific fitment for side cases from the factory or aftermarket, you need to investigate potential exhaust-clearance issues before buying and mounting cases. Scooter exhaust pipes usually pivot with the engine, so you need to ensure the pipe will not hit the side case.

Soft Saddlebags

Saddlebags can be pretty useful for the right person. The easy on and off nature of saddlebags makes them good for traveling or going to the office where they can quickly be brought in with you. Saddlebags have the disadvantage of being less secure than hard side cases, and usually less waterproof to boot. The same exhaust-clearance issues that exist with hard cases apply equally to saddlebags.

Some saddlebags will mount onto a scooter quite easily. Just open the seat, position the bags, and close the seat. The drawback is that this might hinder your access to your underseat storage, or more annoying, access to your fuel and oil tanks. A handful of enterprising scooter owners do not let this deter them. Instead they whip out the scissors to create access openings for these important and frequently used underseat amenities. However, don't expect to be able to return them if they don't work properly after being hacked up. If you don't know what you're doing, it's best not to attempt it.

Saddlebags on a Derbi Atlantis.

(Photo by Bev Brinson)

Tank Bags and Soft Luggage

Many of the soft bags that work for motorcycles also work well on scooters. Tail packs that fit on motorcycle seats often will also fit on scooters. On some scooters, tank bags and other soft luggage can be placed in the floorboard area and then strapped down. Some bags have specially arranged zippers that allow the bag to expand, accordion style. Others have clear pockets for maps. A few are even specially designed to fit between the seat and leg shield of some maxi-scooters. A few scooter models also have fitted luggage for the underseat compartment. These bags are tailor made to drop right in.

Kick Start

Websites and magazines about motorcycle touring contain a wealth of reviews and information about storage accessories.

As with detachable hard cases, this type of bag would be ideal for long trips or the commute to work because it makes gathering your personal effects quick and efficient.

Racks

While some racks are used as accessories for those who want a scooter with lots of shiny bling, they can also be quite useful for toting stuff around. Some are even available in black for those who find chrome to be too ostentatious. Most fitments are for vintage and manual-shift scooters, but there are options out there for other scooters, too. Rear-mounted racks are the most common, but there are a few that can be attached to the front of the leg shield.

For those with manual-shift scooters, the choices can get a bit overwhelming. Do you go with one that folds down, or one that is static? Is a passenger backrest desired? What about grab handles? How about a spare tire mount? Do you prefer a smaller one that works better with the styling of the scooter, or a larger one that is more utilitarian?

Knowing what you generally plan to carry on your rack and the load rating you would need is a good start for making that decision. Many racks don't have very high load ratings because they alter the weight distribution and handling of your scooter, so be aware of how much you're putting on your scooter and where you're putting it.

If you plan to use your rack for the occasional item, then a fold-down might be appropriate. If you want to use it on a daily basis, a fixed platform rack is probably a better choice. Fold-down racks can vibrate and buzz when not locked into the down position. If that bothers you, then it would definitely be something to bear in mind.

As great as regular bungee cords are for securing stuff to carrying racks, bungee nets are pretty slick and, in some cases, more secure than cords. Bungee nets are less likely to slip out of place, so they tend to be supremely useful for holding irregularly shaped objects (like helmets) that must be fastened down. It never hurts to have a few bungees or a bungee net on hand.

Racks also make excellent platforms for alternative top cases. In the old days, leather roll bags were a pretty common storage device. Piaggio has created one to go with their scooters. Similar ones are also available from SX Appeal and Prima. The new ones are made with modern materials and closures so they are more efficient, convenient, and resistant to the elements than the originals. Baskets, milk crates, and small trunks are other ways that scooterists have carried their worldly goods around with them.

Keep your eyes and mind open and you might find just the thing to use as your own alternative top case. A trip to a helpful hardware store can yield the perfect fasteners to attach your new and unique top case to your rack.

Oil Slick

Load your rack carefully. Heavy items placed at one end of the scooter will change the handling in the same way that a passenger can. Liquid items require special caution. If fluids slosh around a half-empty container while you're riding, it can upset the balance of your scoot.

Sidecars and Trailers

Adding more than two wheels to any motorcycle or scooter dramatically alters its performance and handling dynamics. However, if you're willing to live with the compromises and differences, trailers and sidecars are a way to significantly increase the amount of cargo you can carry.

Scooter-specific trailers have had a few cycles of modest popularity and decline. Currently there are none on the market. Scooter-specific trailers nearly always have one wheel and tilt with the bike. Some motorcycle trailers will work with scooters, but many of them are heavy and are best left to the biggest and most powerful scooters. The biggest hurdle to jump is that very few new scooters have any provision for a trailer hitch.

Vintage scooters and modern-manual shift scooters have some hitch availability. The Vespa ET series has been used to tow small billboard trailers for publicity events. Those parts could potentially be used for small motorcycle trailers. If you have a serious need for a trailer, be prepared to do a lot of looking for all of the pieces to make it happen. It's unlikely you will be able to just go to your local scooter shop and ride off with one an hour later.

Sidecars are more popular for scooters than trailers, but they suffer from the same availability issues. While scooter-size sidecars are available new, they pretty much only fit modern manual-shift and vintage scooters. Though scooter sidecars could likely be adapted to some modern automatic scooters, there are no off-the-shelf solutions at present.

Oil Slick

Sidecars make a two-wheeler handle very differently. You basically have to learn to ride all over again, particularly with regard to turning.

Beverages and Hydration

Thirsty scooterists are always on the lookout for ways to imbibe liquids while riding, whether it's coffee for the morning commute or water for those sunny summer marathon rides. A half-, open-face, or flip-up helmet is pretty much requisite for getting those swigs of caffeine into your mouth and not all over your face. Waiting for a stoplight to sip is also recommended. Few have the coordination to successfully attempt sipping while riding.

If your scooter does not come with a leg-shield basket, you can consider a wide range of cup holders. Marine cup holders for boats commonly have swivel systems and will keep your beverage upright even when you and your scooter are leaning into the corners. Some are suction cup mounted, though they don't stick for very long. The more secure method involves drilling holes and using screws or pop rivets to permanently affix a swiveling cup holder to the inner leg shield. Many scooter owners cringe at the very thought of violating their pristine bodywork with drill bits, and if drilling through a steel panel, rust can form where bare metal is exposed. It's certainly not something to do impulsively. Some owners have fitted cup holders with strong magnets. Others have gone to the hardware store and looked high and low to find just the right thing to clamp a beverage holder to their crash bars.

A *hydration pack* is another way to gulp on the run. Unlike with a cup holder, you can actually keep sipping as you ride. The mouthpieces also fit under some full-face helmets, though not all. However, they aren't really suitable for hot beverages. So your extra-tall skinny vanilla latte with Madagascar cinnamon will need to find other accommodations for the ride. For some icy cold water to keep you cool while on the long ride at a mid-summer scooter rally, it's hard to beat the convenience and ease of taking a swig whenever you desire.

def•i•ni•tion
A **hydration pack** is a backpack with a pouch for liquids and a hose and mouthpiece for consuming them while on the go. Some even offer insulation.

As a disclaimer, it is inadvisable to drink intoxicating beverages before or during riding. Riding has enough hazards when sober, so you really need to keep your faculties about you and wait until later to knock back a few.

Windshields

Want a little more top speed, more comfortable cold-weather riding, and a less blustery ride? A windshield can make your scooter faster, lower wind chill, and smooth the flow of air. Want a slower top speed and unpredictable handling in cross winds? Probably not, but a windshield can make that happen, too. Picking the right windshield is a series of compromises, just like picking your scooter was. As a new or prospective scooter rider, you've already figured out that bigger isn't always better, and that compact can be just the thing. In the end, the right windshield for you will be determined by your goals and the conditions you ride in.

Most maxi-scooters such as the Suzuki Burgman shown here include a windshield.

(Photo Courtesy of Suzuki)

Large

If your primary goal is to stay warm while riding in chilly weather, then a tall windshield might be just what you're looking for. This is especially true if you don't routinely deal with high winds and gusts.

Any windshield has the possibility of acting like a sail, with tall ones being most susceptible. Normally, a crosswind will just blow the entire bike. That can be scary and puts demands even on an alert and attentive rider to stay in the lane and on the road. A tall windshield not only adds surface area that can catch the wind, but it places it all on the steering system. On a gusty day you can be tossed about like driftwood on a rough sea. The headset can shake and the steering can get wobbly. In some cases, the only way to safely ride is to slow down to the point that the wind isn't snagging your steering. If you don't heed that kind of warning, your ride can end disastrously.

The other negative is that a larger windshield will usually lower your top speed. Then again, with the potential instability issues, you might find your top speed effectively reduced in the interest of safe riding, more than you imagined.

If you don't encounter high or gusting winds and most of your riding is slow, then a tall windshield is perfect for keeping away a chill. Hand guards are one nice thing that big windshields often have. They deflect a lot of wind away from your fingers to make your gloves more effective at keeping your fingers warm and flexible. A few smaller screens do have them, and universal hand guards are also available that can be installed separately. Wanting a bit of aerodynamic deflection around your hands need not doom you to having a sail rivaling that of a schooner perched atop your headset.

Medium

Mid-size windshields can be a nice all-around compromise between redirecting the flow of air and not being caught in gusts, but it's all about context. A rider in a location with turbulent winds still might notice some grab in a crosswind. On a gusty day, he or she might still have to slow down significantly to maintain control of the scooter.

A medium shield may or may not have an impact on top speed. Depending on the actual size of the screen, the aerodynamics of the scooter, and other issues, the top speed might be a little better, a little worse, or might not change at all. There are a number of variables with medium screens, primarily because an 8-inch and 13-inch model would both be regarded as medium.

Small (or Fly Screens)

Fly screens often look too short to really be useful, but for many riders they are the best choice.

Though they may not be very big, fly screens are the only windshields that actually increase top speed pretty consistently on all makes and models of scooter. Basically, they clean up the aerodynamics and divert the blast of air off the chest and up toward a rider's helmet. This is particularly useful on scooters with large leg shields. Often they will direct a lot of pressure onto the rider's chest, which can lead to fatigue. There are a few such scooters I would not own without at least a good fly screen. If you prefer an open-face or half-helmet, there can occasionally be compatibility issues, but with a full-face helmet it's typically not really noticeable.

Though a fly screen may not create a perfectly calm and turbulence-free riding environment, that's really not possible on a two-wheeled, open vehicle. Even if it were possible, it's debatable how desirable that would be. Much of the fun of riding is feeling the wind and being out in the open. A fly screen does a good job of leaving that aspect of the ride intact while making it more comfortable for a longer period of time, and it's a rare scooterist who would turn down an increase in top speed.

Other Considerations

Quality varies among windshields. Some are well designed and others are not. Some have excellent hardware and install easily while others take much more work.

One other quality issue to look for is the thickness and uniformity of the plastic. That and the curvature of the windshield itself really affect the optical properties. Some screens really do distort things, particularly at the upper edge. The upper edge of a windshield being right in your line of sight will probably drive you crazy and distract you from riding safely.

Mixing polarized sunglasses with windshields is a bad idea. Doubling up on polarizing filters creates psychedelic colors and shapes. Though quite interesting, they can really hinder a rider's ability to see important things like cars and pedestrians. The effect is amplified as the sun descends, so if you use a windshield, it's best to leave the polarized lenses at home or in the car, and have a set of normal ones with the scooter.

If you can see the windshield you're interested in before buying, it's an opportunity you should take full advantage of. If you can have someone hold it up to your bike so you can see how everything lines up, even better. You will be less surprised by the result than if you pull a windshield out of a box, install it, and discover that it does not make you happy at all. Often, it isn't an option, so it's important to try to do your homework as best you can.

Know your riding habits and local conditions. Read professional and owner reviews of the screens you like. Also ask about the return and exchange policy of the vendor you order from. Even if the item is not returnable, you can often sell it off on a message board to another owner. Though you will still pay out of pocket, you can at least reduce the cost by selling it to someone else and then contribute your feedback to the scooter community.

Beyond Windshields

Grip wind deflectors are available separately from windshields and can really make a difference in cold-weather riding. These are commonly available for touring motorcycles and big cruisers, but some can be adapted to scooters.

The aftermarket has also created leg-shield widening extensions for some scooter models to help increase the bubble of calm air around the rider. The most common fitments are for maxi-scooters to make them better as long-distance touring machines.

Bags

Almost as important as the storage attached to the bike is the storage that the rider can wear. Many bags have been designed with riders in mind, like innovative strap designs to prevent the bag from shifting around while riding. In addition to riding-specific bags, there are many bags that are quite suitable for the scooter rider.

Kick Start

Trying on a bag with gear can prevent unexpected complications later on. It's embarrassing to find that you can't put on a bag because it's incompatible with your riding jacket or helmet. Also, it's a good idea to load it up and see how comfortable it is while standing and sitting.

Courier

Many styles of courier and messenger bags work well on scooters, but some are more suitable than others. It's important to have anything attached to your person strapped down securely. Many messenger bags offer additional straps to secure the bag. A sudden shift of weight on two wheels can be pretty unsettling when cruising down a straight road. When blasting through a corner it can have far more serious consequences.

Messenger bags from Chrome, Timbuk2, and others will often have a waist strap that prevents the bag from flopping around. The Roadgear MultiTasker can be worn like a messenger bag, or more like a backpack.

Padded shoulder straps can often help spread the load and make a bag more comfortable to wear for miles on end. Some of them also offer padded compartments for laptops. While they might be helpful in slow crashes, they may not prevent damage at higher speeds. For bags that don't have padding, laptop sleeves that can slip into other bags are available from a number of companies.

When looking for a courier bag, anything that is intended for bicycle use would probably work pretty well on a scooter. The same concepts of quality and comfort apply. A really good bag should be made of abrasion-resistant materials and should have some resistance to water.

Look for sturdy stitching and rugged closures to help keep your cargo from getting out of the bag while zipping along.

Reflectivity is another feature that can help you narrow down your options a bit. 3M Scotchlite reflective trim (or similar) is something to look for.

Fit and comfort are also important. It's not a bad idea to go try on the bags, and actually fill them with a few of your usual items to see how they feel. If you have a regular riding jacket, it wouldn't hurt to bring that along. Often products can interact in funny ways you would not imagine prior to using them in combination. Sure, it's a pain to lug your jacket along, but so is going back to the store to return something that doesn't work.

Backpacks

As mentioned in the intro to this chapter, there are a number of products that were not designed for riding, but have many features that lend themselves to it. When shopping for backpacks, look around through the lens of what you need or want while riding your scooter and you will be amazed at how many products pop out that you previously had never given a second thought. Camping and sporting goods stores can be excellent places to start.

Though most any backpack will work on a scooter, some offer interesting benefits and features. For example, the Axio Hardpack line of backpacks has a hard outer shell and is thoroughly padded to help protect electronic equipment. The Lid Lugger Max has a pouch for your helmet and is specially designed to prevent discomfort and fatigue while riding. Tour Master makes a backpack that is similar in its helmet-gobbling abilities.

Other bags, like the Voltaic Solar backpack, were not intended for riding but have interesting features that some riders like. Being able to harness the sun while you're out riding and to use that energy to charge up your personal electronics is an interesting concept. It comes with an array of charging outputs for a variety of products, from cell phones to personal music players.

As with messenger bags, comfort is a key issue with backpacks. If you aren't riding comfortably, you probably aren't riding safely either due to the fatigue or the distraction caused by being uncomfortable. Trying things out with loads and your safety gear is possibly even more important with backpacks. They require a certain range of motion to throw on and remove. Armored jackets can often make some of those motions a little more difficult, and backpack straps don't always slide smoothly over anti-abrasive materials.

What kind of routine you have when getting ready to ride factors prominently in what you might decide to wear and carry. Some backpacks are nearly impossible to put on while wearing a helmet. Quality and design are other issues to look at seriously. If the strap adjusters leave a lot of excess strapping dangling around, you might want to reconsider or look for a way to secure them. At 60 miles per hour or more, they can really start whipping around. If they have hard plastic pieces at the ends, you might find little bruises along your ribs after a ride.

How things zip up, and whether flaps will act as air scoops, are other factors to keep in mind. Durable and abrasion-resistant materials with sturdy construction techniques are highly recommended. Dependable water resistance really weighs heavily on your mind when you get caught out in a shower on the way home with a lot of important work documents or electronics on your back. Reflective material and things like waist straps and well-padded shoulder straps help separate regular backpacks from really good backpacks for riding.

GPS Systems

Motorcycle-specific GPS systems are the new, hot gadget to have. With the capability to show you your top speed, perform automatic routing, give you audible directions over a Bluetooth headset, and store many destinations, it's not hard to see why.

Many handheld and automotive GPS systems have been pressed into riding duty by motorcycle and scooter riders over the past few years, but recently big GPS manufacturers have released models that are two-wheel-specific. With lessons learned from marine applications, the motorcycle-specific models are more water resistant than the handheld ones. Easy on-and-off mounting systems help fasten the unit securely to the bike but also allow easy user removal to prevent theft and vandalism.

Garmin claims its new Zumo to be readable in bright conditions, glove friendly, and resistant to vibration. With an optional antenna, it is also

XM capable. TomTom's RIDER supports Bluetooth and can provide audio prompts into your helmet. It has a feature that increases and decreases the ear volume based on the speed you're riding. It also has an anti-glare screen and is supposed to be glove friendly.

Electronic Accessories

Motorcycle electronics can make a bike safer, more fun, and more comfortable by enhancing lighting, warming your hands, and powering accessory devices.

Stereos

Some scooterists are diehard music fiends who simply cannot live without their tunes. Many of them have built their own stereo systems for their scooters. Japanese scooter customizers seem to consider a mobile audio system to be an obligatory part of any custom scooter. The majority of stereo installations are one-offs created by owners because there are only a handful of readily available systems.

Scooterworks carries an audio system composed of speakers, an amplifier, and the wiring to integrate your MP3 player into the glove box of your Stella, Bajaj, or Vespa P-series scooter. Sportique Scooters built a Stella with a sidecar rig that has a complete entertainment system in it with iPod connectivity, CD, DVD, and radio-receiver head unit and several potent speakers that can rock out the parking area of any scooter rally.

Pictures have even circulated on the Internet of a project a design student did to create an electric scooter with a deeply integrated audio system. To take it one step further, it actually uses an iPod as the ignition key.

> **Oil Slick** ——————————————————————
> The charging systems on most scooters were not intended to power toys and gizmos that suck down the juice. High-power accessories like stereo systems will require more frequent battery charging, or possibly even auxiliary batteries.

Auxiliary Power Ports

Most electronics shops offer all the parts you would need to install a 12-volt auxiliary power port into your scooter. Whether it has the power to spare is another matter. This kind of project really isn't for those without previous electrical experience. For those who can figure it out, an auxiliary power port can offer the ability to charge electronics or even power a heated vest or gloves for those chilly rides.

Heated Grips

Winter riding can be made much more pleasant with the addition of heated grips, particularly when combined with hand deflectors or handlebar muffs. As with auxiliary power ports, they require wiring knowledge to install properly. If you're not capable of doing it yourself, your scooter shop or independent motorcycle mechanic could probably do the job for you.

Drain on the system is another concern to keep in mind, as it is with all other electrical add-ons. It's important to know whether or not your scooter has the electrical output capacity to power the grips and to continue to recharge the battery.

Lighting

Copious quantities of accessory lighting may not be your scene, but there are functional and low-key upgrades that can be done to improve the lighting of most scooters.

Auxiliary lights can help brighten the road and illuminate parts of the road that your headlight doesn't quite reach. Lighting up the edge of the road is especially welcome for those who do a lot of riding on the back roads anytime after the sun drops below the horizon. Being able to see the critters at the roadside before they dart out in front of you can make all the difference between a near miss and an accident. For those who dislike the Mod look, there are small lights that can be attached to fork tubes.

Daylight riding also can call for lighting upgrades for increased visibility to those around you. Headlight modulators work with your high beam on; they flash the headlight to help oncoming and turning traffic see you. Brake-light upgrades are also common. High-intensity LED bulbs are an option that many turn to for brighter brake lights that use less electricity. Flashers are also available for brake lights to increase visibility to those behind you.

The Least You Need to Know

+ A world of storage options is available for scooters.

+ Bigger is not always better when it comes to windshields.

+ Riding bags make commuting easier.

+ Motorcycle electronics can make a bike safer, more fun, and more comfortable.

Chapter 10

"La Dolce Vita"– Living It

In This Chapter

- ◆ Scooter subcultures
- ◆ Extreme riding
- ◆ Rallies and events
- ◆ Scooter clubs

With the increase in popularity of scooters, scooter-related sub-cultures have grown and become more varied. From the Mods to the new Twist-and-Go groups, you can find a club that organizes group activities you can participate in. Whether it's a weekend ride, a trip to an ice cream shop, or a fundraising event, there is something for everyone, from the casual weekend rider to the devoted scooterist who is hopelessly addicted.

Scooter Subcultures

Scooters have spawned a number of subcultures. The Mods are probably the best known. Often seen wearing suits or other chic clothing, they like to trick out their rides with crash bars, ridiculous numbers of lights, and rearview mirrors by the dozen. Their motorcycle riding enemies were the Rockers, who usually sported slicked-back hair, and often were clad in leather jackets.

Other groups include skinheads (often the nonracist ones referred to as Skinheads Against Racial Prejudice, or S.H.A.R.P.s). Scooterboys are a subculture that sprung up in the 1980s. As with the Mods and scooter skins, the Scooterboys originated in the U.K. and they are still concentrated primarily there. The influence of these three groups can be seen in the United States, mostly among the vintage scene. However, there are those nostalgic for the Mod look who are applying it to new scooters.

All subcultures have their own music (nearly all scooter subcultures have strong ties to specific genres of music, with soul, reggae, ska, and punk being well-established favorites), their own fashion, and their own value systems. Scooter subcultures are about as difficult to join as any other underground group. While most members of these subcultures have no problem associating with the mainstream scooter rider, they won't automatically accept just anybody as one of their own. Most people will appreciate your being who you are instead of trying to pretend and be a poser in a group that really is not your thing.

Oil Slick

It's best not to make assumptions and label people based on stereotypes. A scooter rider with tattoos and closely cropped hair might not be a skinhead. The guy who rides in a suit may not be a mod. And either of them might be offended if you call them a skin or mod. If people strongly identify with a subculture, they will let you know.

Commuting

Avid commuters are another breed of scooter owner. Many of these daily riders can be seen trekking to work not only in fair weather but also in conditions that are hot, cold, rainy, or otherwise unpleasant.

Some do it because they want to save money, use less gasoline, or make socio-political statements. The most serious among them typically ride because they find that their day consists of two rides punctuated by work. These are the people you will see out and about when it's just barely above freezing, on rainy days, or on that mid-July day with a record-high temperature.

Super-commuters are the type of riders who break in their scooters the first week they own them. They love to brag about how they can fit a week's worth of groceries on their scooters. Their cars usually sit around gathering dust as the scooter does the duty of daily transportation. Some of them are so addicted to riding that they will find scenic routes to work, or any other destinations they may have in mind. The hardcore scooter riders really exemplify the attitude behind the phrase "Live to ride, ride to live."

Extreme Scootering

What hobby would be complete without people trying to one up each other? Scooterists have found several ways to cement their status within the scooter world as being tough, enthusiastic, dedicated, or perhaps even a little crazy.

Racing

Since the dawn of time, human beings have felt the need for speed. While it may have started with the simple foot race, as we have acquired new toys, we have always found new ways to determine which one is really the fastest. Bragging is one of the most beloved pastimes of our species, and scooterists are in no way alien to the concept.

There are racing-sanctioning bodies scattered about the country that schedule and supervise scooter road racing on race tracks. With classes for stock and modified scooters, there is something for everyone. Rules vary by region, but all require a few safety preparations be made to the bike. Riders must be clad in a specified minimum level of protective gear, usually including a set of leathers and a Snell-approved full-face helmet. Sanctioning bodies typically require that your scooter have specific bolts safety-wired so they will not come loose. Nyloc nuts are required on other parts, and a few items must be taped (like headlights) before venturing onto the track. Getting your scoot on the track is quite inexpensive as far as racing goes.

Racers lean over and drag knees to corner during a race at the Nationals held in Denver.

(Photo by Bev Brinson)

Mid-American Scooter Sports (MASS) serves the Midwest and has held races in Ohio and Missouri, as well as the renowned Road America track in Elkhart Lake, Wisconsin. The Eastern Scooter Racing Association (ESRA) holds races throughout the East. They have held events at tracks like Virginia International Raceway and Summit Point. The American Scooter Racing Association (ASRA), based in California, is the oldest scooter-racing group in the United States, and they have held races in Las Vegas, Nevada, and at tracks like Streets of Willow.

Scootrivia

Road racing on twisty tracks is only one form of scooter racing. Drag racing has become popular among European scooterists. In the United States, scooters are often used as pit bikes for automobile and motorcycle racing. These sometimes get raced for fun at the end of the day.

Cross-Country Events

Every other year a group of very tough scooter owners do what most Americans consider inconceivable: they ride their scooters from sea to shining sea in a very long endurance race. The Scooter Cannonball has a limited number of slots open to riders who have more iron in their backsides than most scooter or motorcycle riders will ever dream of having. With a lower and upper displacement of 125cc and 251cc, respectively, the Scooter Cannonball may not be the fastest transcontinental race, but it is a challenge that inspired very serious competition in the inaugural race in 2004. At the time of this book's writings, the next event is gearing up for what looks like an even more fiercely contested race.

Cold-Weather Challenge

For those who won't let a little frostbite get in the way of a good time, what could be better than trying to ride farther in colder temperatures than anyone else? The winner is chosen on the basis of miles ridden and temperature. For instance, a distance of 10 miles at 13°F (-10.5°C) beats a 1-mile ride at 11°F (-11.5°C). Data is submitted to a website on the honor system, with the temperature backed by a credible source like a weather report or a photo of you and your scooter by a bank clock. There is no absolute zero for the two-wheeled equivalent of the Polar Bear Club.

Rallies

The family reunions of the scootering world, rallies are great events for socializing with others who have a fever for scooters. Rallies can greatly differ in activities and demographics, but all of them use scooters as a pretext for an opportunity to get together with old friends, and make a few new ones.

There are two broad types of rallies. Camping rallies are a lot like they sound. A bunch of scooters arrive at a campsite of some sort. People sleep in their tents or vehicles. And in between rides there is usually a lot of partying. City rallies tend to be more structured and have several scheduled activities. Participants usually stay in hotels or lodge with friends in the host city. Both are fun and offer the opportunities to form lifelong friendships with people from all over the country. It's also great to meet the community elders who have an encyclopedic knowledge of all things scooter-related and who carried the torch that kept the scene alive when scooters weren't as popular as they are now.

The majority of city rallies tend to follow the same basic template. Friday kicks off the weekend with a meet-and-greet where participants show up and hang out for a little while. It's also usually when *rally packs* are distributed. After or during the Friday meet-and-greet, there may or may not be an organized dinner. Typically there is a party later Friday evening, often at a bar that is frequented by the club hosting the rally. These parties are often known for going very late into the night, even at rallies where Saturday-morning activities start early.

def·i·ni·tion

A **rally pack** is a goody bag that contains a schedule of events, maps, sponsor information, and a number of little goodies and promo items from rally sponsors. At some rallies the rally patch and t-shirt are part of the pack.

Originally equestrian events where horses and riders made timed runs through obstacle courses, **gymkhana** were once reasonably common in Great Britain. Scooterists use the word to describe a timed obstacle course that is performed on a scooter.

Saturday activities often start out with some kind of breakfast. After that, the group usually rides to a location where several activities will take place. During this time the judging for the scooter show often takes place. Categories often award owners with trophies for things like Best Vintage Vespa, Best Lambretta, Best Modern Manual, Best Automatic, Best Rat Bike, Best Custom, People's Choice, and so on. Which awards are being given largely depends on the club who organized the rally. An exclusively vintage club will normally focus on vintage scooters and have trophies for specific models. A club with a more diverse collection of scooters might offer awards in several very broad categories.

Around the time the judging is going on, the *gymkhana* will often be getting under way. Those who sign up to participate in the gymkhana are in for a wild ride over obstacles requiring some serious moxie. Ramps, bridges, and jumps are common to most gymkhanas. Weaving through cone slaloms, making tight figure-eights, and riding in small circles are other time-honored traditions for trick riders. Aside from the basics, many organizers will add extra-difficult stunts for daredevils to perform. Riding over teeter-totters is not at all uncommon, and zooming up a ramp into the bed of a pickup truck is a spectacular way to finish a course. Water hazards also test the skill of participants. Several clubs also have their own traditions that they add. A few highlights include having riders go under limbo bars, shoot water guns, carry eggs or other delicate objects from one place to another, or stop their scooters and balance without putting feet down.

A group ride during the Mile High Mayhem Rally heads out for an afternoon of riding and a picnic.

(Photo by Bev Brinson)

A rider's run through the course is timed and judges follow the rider to score points for completing obstacles and subtract for putting feet down, hitting obstacles, or otherwise not properly completing the course. The rider's speed is reflected in the final score. Riding in a gymkhana is a potentially dangerous activity, and it is rare to go to one where nobody drops a scooter. If participating is a little too risky or bold for you, it can be just as fun to pull up a good seat and watch talented riders. Watching riders without much talent can be fun, too.

Slow races are usually next on the agenda. As contests of will and balance, slow races pit two riders against one another. The first one to the finish line loses; the first person to put a foot down also loses. With each race the winner goes on to face other winners.

Top-notch slow race riders can often make their bikes move barely an inch at a time. When two highly skilled riders meet on the asphalt battlefield, the event becomes a super-slow-motion game of chicken. Psych-outs, faking, and other subtle forms of distraction, deception, and intimidation are fair game to use against one's opponent. As the tension runs higher, it often looks as though riders will let themselves fall to the ground before conceding defeat by putting down a stabilizing foot. At the last possible second the handlebars are turned and the rider's weight shifts to prevent a wicked fall.

Slow races are great events because anyone who can ride has the basic skills to participate. Winning definitely takes talent and practice, but even doing one or two rounds before being beaten is a lot of fun.

After the morning activities there is usually a ride to a lunch destination. After the lunch, the group splits up for two separate rides. Those with smaller, slower scooters usually can opt for the slower ride, which often takes the form of a city tour. The longer, fast rides often head out of town on a quest to carve up the best winding roads the host city has to offer. As the rides draw to a close, rally goers often get some free time to catch a nap or chill out before meeting up for dinner. After dinner there may be a short evening ride that meanders through town on the way to the Saturday night party spot. Those who did go and take naps may find themselves staying up until the wee hours.

Sundays typically are when awards get presented. In addition to the trophies for the best bikes in each category, the winners of the gymkhana and slow race usually get some hardware to take home. Some clubs also give trophies to the rally jackass or class clown. What better way is there to thank someone for risking his or her own health and safety for the amusement of others all weekend long?

Raffles are a long-standing rally tradition. Organizers get sponsors to donate items for the raffle, which are then given away. The money from the raffle either goes into the coffers of the club to help them put on the event next year, or in some cases it goes to a local charity that the host club likes to support.

Some raffles are known for having very extravagant prizes. At the 2006 Amerivespa rally, a grand total of six scooters were raffled off. Many large rallies often get a scooter or two for the raffle, and some smaller ones manage to offer a scoot from time to time. Riding gear makes up most of the other big prizes. Helmets, jackets, and other assorted goodies flow like wine. Gift certificates related to various sponsors are another great prize that is often given away.

Kick Start _____

Scoot.net is the site for all things related to scooter rallies. It has the most comprehensive calendar of American rallies, and participants can upload their pictures after the event.

Clubs

Scooter clubs are a great way to learn more about scooters, improve your riding skills, and make new friends. Successful clubs tend to start out small, when a few people start doing activities together that attract others. As activity participation grows, the groups tend to formalize a bit and eventually a club is born.

Many modern clubs form around riding. Vintage-oriented clubs often tend to be focused on scoot culture and the chance to wrench and tinker. Clubs form for a variety of reasons, but they thrive when compatible people get together and find they like hanging out.

There is no formula for starting a club that works 100 percent of the time. If there is no club or scooter scene in your area, the best way to get something started is to talk to your local scooter shops about wanting to ride with other people. Set up a website; a group on Yahoo!; or post flyers with your name, number, and e-mail address around places you see scooters.

Once you meet a few people who like to do group rides, you can start meeting up regularly at a certain time and place. As word gets out, more people will often show up. As people discover they have other common interests, they begin to participate in other activities together. If a few people all love a band, they might go to a concert together. These kinds of bonding experiences make a club stronger and eventually more people will start showing up.

All clubs that have any longevity figure out early on who they are and what they want to do as a group. Clubs that try to be everything to everyone often fall apart. Clubs that are too exclusive don't grow. Clubs that let just anyone in can run into problems with not having a specific focus. No matter what focus a club chooses, it needs to reflect the desires of the members, and the club's activities should reflect their purpose. A club name, patch, officer hierarchy, and other trappings of established clubs are not really necessary initially, and without the right foundation to build those things on, they usually won't last.

Many clubs have direct or de facto sponsorship from their local scooter shops. Many clubs use the local scooter shop as a meet-up point and official or unofficial clubhouse. Some shops give discounts to club members on parts, accessories, clothing, and safety gear. Scooter shops also sponsor events for their local scooter communities, often in conjunction with scooter clubs. Sportique Scooters of Denver, Colorado, periodically hosts outdoor scoot-in movies at their shop. Scooter World Kansas City is a primary sponsor of a winter food-drive event organized by the Mad Toto Scooter Club called Will Scoot 4 Food, where food is donated to Harvesters and then transported to their location primarily by scooter in January or February. Many scooter shops are strong members of their community and are great contact points for meeting other scooter riders.

Online

There are few facets of American life that the Internet has not touched. Getting connected with scooter people and activities is easier than ever with the popularity of online scooter groups. There are message boards, e-mail groups, and blogs on any scooter-related topic you can imagine.

Yahoo! offers a huge variety of groups, and seems to be the best place to search for brand- and model-specific online communities. Not only could you find a group for the Yamaha Vino on Yahoo! Groups, there is a thriving group of women. If vintage is your thing, you can find a group entirely devoted to small-frame Vespas like the Primavera. Many local scooter clubs also use these groups as their official club message boards. If you are looking for a club in your city, these groups should be on your list of places to look.

The Scooter BBS (www.scooterbbs.com) is the great granddaddy of scooter message boards at the ripe old age of 10. The BBS has been subdivided into several sections. The oldest is the original International Scooterist BBS, which is focused on vintage and manual-shift scooters. The International New Scooter BBS is a spinoff of the original BBS and is for new, modern, and primarily automatic scooters. Over the years, both sides have been excellent resources for scooterists of all stripes. The Spam section of the board features scooters for sale and wanted ads posted by board users.

As mentioned above, scoot.net has the most comprehensive calendar of American scooter rallies, and it also is the repository for rally-related images. In addition it features loads of classified ads for scooters and parts for sale or wanted.

There are also several brand-specific message boards for new scooters. Modern Vespa is the site for all things related to new Vespa and Piaggio scooters. Modern Buddy is their sister site and is a resource for owners of the automatic scooters from the Genuine Scooter Company. Getting linked up with like-minded scooter owners is just a click away these days.

Finding parts and accessories is also simple. Most scooter dealers are online, and scooter parts retailers are as well. The only trick is knowing who to go to for which parts. However, you can do some looking around and then ask people on your model-specific discussion board for advice on the best place to buy whatever it is that you need.

Scooters Abroad

Americans have been a bit out of the loop on the whole scooter thing for a while, but in the rest of the world, scooters are so commonplace that they are everywhere. Travel throughout Europe or Southeast Asia and you will see scooters galore.

Scooter Rental

Even cooler than seeing scoots everywhere is renting one while you're on a trip. While in other countries, you are likely to have the chance to ride scooters not sold in this country. If you do, take it. Going abroad is supposed to be about doing things you can't do at home and learning about things you don't see normally.

On the Greek Isles, rental scooters are one of the most common ways for tourists to get around. In Italy there are tour companies that arrange group tours through Tuscany and other parts of Italy on new Vespas.

In Asia, renting a scooter is more like renting a car in the United States. You are not renting a touristy toy. Instead you are renting the transportation appliance that everyone else uses. In Taiwan, the scooters you can rent are usually not pretty, though they do work. Be sure not to make the mistake of asking to rent a pair of Grand Vista 250s.

The shop owner might laugh aloud at your suggestion of renting her family's private scooter. If you ride through the Taiwanese countryside, try not to gawk too much when you see an older woman herding oxen on a scooter.

The one constant no matter where you go and ride is to learn the rules of the road before embarking on any kind of two-wheeled adventure. In other parts of the world, traffic is not quite as formal or orderly as it is in America. Things tend to go with the flow, but until you understand the flow of things you are putting yourself in danger. One rule that seems to follow universally is that the bigger vehicle almost always has the right of way.

Foreign Scooter Literature

Scooters are in a period of revival in the United States, but we have some serious catching up to do with our counterparts across the pond. Scooter culture, tuning, and customization in Europe and the U.K. are in a completely different league than they are here.

British magazines like Scootering show the level of enthusiasm for building and displaying wildly customized scooters. The images no doubt serve as inspiration for vintage-scooter lovers in the United States who like to dream big about how they could so completely personalize their rides. *Twist and Go* magazine is all about new automatics, and focuses heavily on performance tuning. European sport-scooter lovers have probably already tried most of the performance-tuning goodies that have only a small knowledge base stateside. The British are passionate about their scooters and they have compiled a wealth of information that is definitely worth importing.

The Least You Need to Know

- There is a vast scooter community with a niche for everyone.
- Riding is highly addictive.
- Scooter rallies are a great place to meet interesting people.
- Joining a club has many benefits, including people to ride with.
- The Internet is an abundant source of scooter info.

Appendix A

Current Models

Following is a list of distributors and models that meet EPA/DOT requirements. While we have made every attempt to be as accurate as possible, all information is subject to change.

Aprilia (www.ApriliaUSA.com)

Scarabeo 50 4T

Engine	Horizontal single-cylinder four-stroke; overhead cam; forced air cooling, conforms to emission control standards
Bore × Stroke	1.5"×1.6" (39×41.8 mm)
Displacement	49.9cc
Compression Ratio	11.5–12:1
Cooling	Forced air cooling
Carburetor	Keihin 20 mm carburetor
Gear Box	air cooled, auto variator
Clutch	centrifugal
Frame	Single spar with double cradle in high strength steel
F Suspension	Hydraulic fork; wheel travel 80 mm
R Suspension	Hydraulic monoshock; wheel travel 80 mm

Aprilia (www.ApriliaUSA.com) (continued)

Scarabeo 50 4T

F Brake	220 mm stainless steel disc; caliper with two opposed
R Brake	30 mm pistons, 140 mm drum
F/R Tire	80/80×16"/90/80×16"
L×W×H	75"×27.8"×50"
Seat Height	30.7"
Wheelbase	49.4"
Fuel Capacity	2.1 gallons, including 0.26 gallon reserve
Dry Weight	165 lbs (74.8 kg)
Colors	Main Blue, Venice White
MSRP	$2,499

Scarabeo 250

Engine	Single-cylinder, four-stroke, liquid cooled, SOHC, 4-valve, catalyzed exhaust
Bore × Stroke	2.8"×2.4"
Displacement	244cc
Compression Ratio	11:1
Carburetor	Keihin 29 mm carburetor
Gear Box	Automatic variator
Clutch	Automatic centrifugal
Frame	High-strength tubular steel single spar with double cradle
F Suspension	36 mm hydraulic fork; wheel travel 110 mm
R Suspension	Engine acting as swing arm, secured to the frame by two linkages on radial vibration dampers; laterally mounted double-acting hydraulic monoshock with spring preload adjustment 260 mm stainless steel disc; floating caliper with three 25 mm pistons
F Brake	260 mm stainless steel disc; floating caliper with three 25 mm pistons
R Brake	240 mm stainless steel disc; caliper with two 32 mm opposed pistons
F/R Tire	110/80×16"/130/80×16"

Scarabeo 250

L×W×H	79.9"×28.3"×52.3"
Seat Height	31.5"
Wheelbase	55.7"
Fuel Capacity	2.5 gallons, including 0.5 gallon reserve
Dry Weight	463 lbs
Colors	Diamond Gray, Peak Gray
MSRP	$4,999

Scarabeo 500

Engine	Liquid cooled single-cylinder four-stroke, single overhead cam (SOHC), 4-valve, catalytic exhaust
Bore × Stroke	3.6"×0.2"
Displacement	460cc
Compression Ratio	10.5:1
Gear Box	Automatic variator
Clutch	Automatic centrifugal
Frame	High-strength tubular steel trellis frame with double cradle for high flexural and torsional rigidity
F Suspension	40 mm hydraulic fork; wheel travel 100 mm
R Suspension	Engine acting as swing arm, coupled to frame by two linkages mounted on radial vibration dampers; two gas-charged double-acting hydraulic shock absorbers with spring preload adjustment; wheel travel 110 mm
F Brake	Twin 260 mm stainless steel discs; floating calipers with two pistons; integral braking system with pressure distribution valve, assisted by FTE's CORA system with ABS and servo-assistance
R Brake	220 mm stainless steel disc; floating caliper with two opposed pistons; integral braking system with pressure distribution valve
F/R Tire	110/80×16"/140/70×16"
L×W×H	90.9"×30.9"×56.5"
Seat Height	31.5"

continues

Aprilia (www.ApriliaUSA.com) (continued)

Scarabeo 500

Wheelbase	63.2"
Fuel Capacity	4.5 gallons
Dry Weight	425 lbs
Colors	Diamond Gray, Lead Gray
MSRP	$7,399

SR 50

Engine	Liquid cooled horizontal single-cylinder two-stroke
Bore × Stroke	1.6"×1.5"
Displacement	49.9cc
Compression	12.1:1
Cooling	Forced air cooling
Carburetor	Dell'Orto PHVA 17.5
Gear Box	Automatic variator
Clutch	Automatic centrifugal dry clutch
Frame	Split single cradle frame in high tensile strength steel tube
F Suspension	Hydraulic fork; wheel travel 90 mm
R Suspension	Engine unit acting as swing arm; frame linkages on two radial silent block mountings; wheel travel 70 mm
F Brake	190 mm stainless steel disc; racing caliper with twin opposed 32 mm pistons
R Brake	190 mm stainless steel disc; racing caliper with twin opposed 30 mm pistons
F/R Tire	130/60×13"/130/60×13"
L×W×H	73"×27.8"×44"
Seat Height	32.3" (820 mm)
Wheelbase	50.8" (1,290 mm)
Fuel Capacity	1.8 gallons (7 Liters)
Dry Weight	397 lbs (180 kg)
Colors	Aprilia Black, Mirror Silver
MSRP	$2,999

Bajaj/Argo USA (www.BajajUSA.com)

Auto Rickshaw

Forward Gears	Twist grip operated, left hand
Reverse Gears	Lever engaged
Accelerator	Twist grip operated, right hand
Clutch	Lever operated, left hand
Brakes – F/R	Pedal operated, right foot
System	12 V, AC + DC, 100 watts
Battery	14 A.h
Length/Width	103"/51"
Height	67"
Wheel Base	79"
Bed Size	Seats 3 plus driver
Door opening	40" h, 28" w
Maximum Total Weight	1389 lbs
Climbing Ability Max	19 percent
MSRP	$6,499

Chetak

Engine Type	145cc four-stroke
Transmission	4-speed manual
Cooling	Forced air
Dry Weight	253 lbs
Seat Height	31"
Fuel Capacity	1.32 gallons
Front/Rear Wheel	3.5×10"/3.5×10"
Brakes Front/Rear	Drum/drum
Carrying Capacity	311 lbs
Color	Ferrari Red, Oxford White, Warm Silver, Misty Jade, Black
MSRP	$2,699

All-steel monocoque chassis, 100 mpg, anti-dive front suspension, electric and kick-start, complete spare tire, 2-year limited warranty

continues

Bajaj/Argo USA (www.BajajUSA.com (continued))

Pick-Up Truck

Forward Gears	Twist grip operated, left hand
Reverse Gears	Lever engaged
Accelerator	Twist grip operated, right hand
Clutch	Lever operated, left hand
Brakes – F/R	Pedal operated, right foot
System	12 V, AC + DC, 100 watts
Battery	14 A.h
Length/Width	100"/54"
Height	67"
Wheel Base	65"
Bed Size	42" d, 49" w, 12" h sides
Door opening	40" h, 28" w
Maximum Total Weight	1697 lbs
Climbing Ability Max	16 percent
MSRP	$6,499

Delivery Van

Forward Gears	Twist grip operated, left hand
Reverse Gears	Lever engaged
Accelerator	Twist grip operated, right hand
Clutch	Lever operated, left hand
Brakes – F/R	Pedal operated, right foot
System	12 V, AC + DC, 100 watts
Battery	14 A.h
Length/Width	104"/47"
Height	68"
Wheel Base	65"
Bed Size	Box size: 50" d, 43" w, 44" h
Door Opening	40" h, 28" w
Maximum Total Weight	1697 lbs
Climbing Ability Max	16 percent
MSRP	$6,899

CF Moto

V3, V5

	CF-250T-V3	*CF250T-V5*
Engine Type	Four-stroke	Four-stroke
cylinders	1	1
Displacement	244cc	244
Bore × Stroke	72 mm×60 mm	72×60
Cooling System	liquid	liquid
Gearbox	CVT	CVT
Front Brake	Disc	Disc
Rear Brake	Disc	Disc
Front Wheel/Tire	100/90-18	100/90-18
Rear Wheel/Tire	150/80-15	150/80-15
Fuel Capacity	12 L	16
Weight	177 kg	164
Colors	Black/Silver	Black/Red
Warranty	12 months	12 months
MSRP	$3,595	$3,295

Daelim (www.DaelimUSA.com)

A-Four-50

L×W×H	70.78"×26.89"×43.58"
Wheel Base	49.61"
Ground Clearance	4.52"
Seat Height	29.52"
Dry Weight	202.6 lbs
Fuel Tank Capacity	1.64 gallons
Brakes F/R	Disc/drum
Tires F/R	120/70-12"/130/70-12"
Suspension F/R	Telescopic fork/damper
System	air cooled, two-stroke
Displacement	49.5cc
Bore × Stroke	1.53"×1.63"
Compression Ratio	6.8:1

continues

Daelim (www.DaelimUSA.com) (continued)

A-Four-50

Carburator Type	PB type
Starting System	Kick/electric
Transmission	V-belt automatic
Ignition System	CDI
Max Power	5.1 ps
Horse Power	3.2 HP
MSRP	$1,790

Daelim E-Five 50 (SJ50A)

L×W×H	70.5"×26.97"×44.48"
Wheel Base	49.61"
Ground Clearance	5.16"
Seat Height	30.51"
Dry Weight	189.42 lbs
Tank Capacity	1.64 gallons
Brakes Front/Rear	Disc/drum
Tires Front/Rear	130/90-10"/130/90-10"
Suspension F/R	Telescopic fork/damper system
Displacement	49.5cc, air cooled, two-stroke
Bore × Stroke	1.53"×1.63"
Compression Ratio	6.8:1
Starting System	Kick/electric
Transmission	V-belt automatic
Ignition System	CDI
Horse Power	3.2 HP
MSRP	$1,790

Cordi 50 (SE50)

L×W×H	66.69"×26.18"×41.46"
Wheel Base	48.31"
Ground Clearance	4.13"
Seat Height	29.33"
Dry Weight	169.76 lbs
Fuel Capacity	1.27 gallons
Brakes Front/Rear	Disc/drum
Tires Front/Rear	90/90-10"/90/90-10"

Cordi 50 (SE50)

Suspension F/R	Telescopic fork/swing arm
System	Air cooled, two-stroke
Displacement	49.5cc
Bore × Stroke	1.57"×1.55"
Compression Ratio	7.3:1
Carburetor Type	PB 35
Starting System	Kick/electric
Transmission	V-belt automatic
Ignition System	CDI
Max Power	5.1 ps
Horse Power	3.2 HP
MSRP	$1,450

Delfino (SH100)

L×W×H	71.26"×26.77"×44.49"
Wheel Base	50.79"
Ground Clearance	4.33"
Seat Height	31.5"
Dry Weight	198.42 lbs
Fuel Capacity	1.9 gallons
Brakes F/R	Disc/drum
Tires F/R	100/90-10"/100/90-10"
Suspension F/R	Telescopic/swing arm
System	air cooled, two-stroke
Displacement	99.7cc
Bore × Stroke	1.99"×1.95"
Compression Ratio	6.9:1
Carburetor Type	PD type
Starting System	Kick/electric
Transmission	V-belt automatic
Ignition System	CDI
Max Power	8.3 ps
Horse Power	8 HP
MSRP	$1,990

continues

Daelim (www.DaelimUSA.com)   (continued)

History 125 (SL125)

Displacement	124.9cc
L×W×H	77.16"×27.68"×48.19"
Wheel Base	53.03"
Ground Clearance	4.33"
Seat Height	30.51"
Dry Weight	271.17 lbs
Fuel Capacity	2.25 gallons
Brakes Front/Rear	Disc/disc
Tires Front/Rear	120/70-12, 130/70-12
Suspension F/R	Telescopic/swing arm
System	air and oil cooled four-stroke—4-valve
Bore × Stroke	2.20"×1.99"
Compression Ratio	11.0:1
Carburetor Type	CV type
Starting System	Kick/electric
Transmission	V-belt automatic
Ignition System	CDI
Max Power	11 ps
Horse Power	11.3 HP
MSRP	$2,490

S2 125, 250

	125 (SQ125)	*250*
L×W×H	83.10"×29.15"×52.75"	83.10"×29.15"×52.75"
Wheel Base	58.3"	58.3"
Ground Clearance	4.72"	4.72"
Seat Height	29.52"	29.52"
Dry Weight	310.5 lbs	341.4 lbs
Fuel Capacity	3.04 gallons	3.04 gallons
Brakes Front/Rear	Disc/disc	Disc/disc
Tires Front/Rear	120/70-12, 130/70-12	120/70-12, 140/60-13
Suspension F/R	Telescopic/swing arm	Telescopic/swing arm
System	Air and oil cooled, four-stroke, 4-Valve	Water cooled, four-stroke, 2-valve
Displacement	124.9cc	249cc

S2 125, 250

Bore × Stroke	2.20"×1.99"	2.86"×2.36"
Compression Ratio	10.8:1	10.3:1
Carburetor Type	Keihin CVK	Keihin CVK
Starting System	Electric	Electric
Transmission	V-belt automatic	V-belt automatic
Ignition System	CDI	CDI
Max Power	12.4 ps	20 ps
Horse Power	12.2 HP	19.7 HP
MSRP	$2,990	$3,990

S5 50

L×W×H	70.67"×27.44"×43.86"
Wheel Base	49.61"
Seat Height	30.12"
Dry Weight	191.8 lbs
Fuel Capacity	1.64 gallons
Brakes Front/Rear	Disc/drum
Tires Front/Rear	120/70-12"/130/70-12"
Suspension F/R	Telescopic fork/damper
System	Air cooled, two-stroke
Displacement	49.5cc
Bore × Stroke	1.53"×1.63"
Compression Ratio	6.8:1
Carburetor Type	PB type
Starting System	Kick/electric
Transmission	V-belt automatic
Max Power	5.1 ps
Horse Power	3.2 HP
MSRP	$1,790

Diamo (www.DiamoUSA.com)

Aero GTX50

Engine	49.5cc four-stroke, air cooled
Brakes Front/Rear	Disc/drum

continues

Diamo (www.DiamoUSA.com)   (continued)

Aero GTX50

LxWxH	73"×26"×46"
Fuel Efficiency	80-100 mpg
Fuel Capacity	2 gallon
Gauges	Fuel Gauge, Odometer, Speedometer
Maximum Load	220 lbs
Max Power	3.5 HP
Seat Height	29"
Start	Electric/kick
Suspension	Front and rear dual shock
Tires Front/Rear	130/60-13"/130/60-13"
Weight	249 lbs
Wheel Base	50"
Colors	Blue, Red, Silver
MSRP	$1,695

Fury 150

Engine	SYM 150cc ceramic cylinder, four-stroke air cooled, Keihin carb
Brakes F/R	Disc/drum
LxWxH	86"×29"×44"
Fuel Efficiency	75-80 mpg
Fuel Capacity	2 gallon
Gauges	Fuel Gauge, LED Indicator Lights, Odometer, Speedometer
Maximum Load	330 lbs
Max Power	9.8 HP
Seat Height	29"
Suspension	Front dual shock, rear mono shock
Tires Front/Rear	130/60-13"/130/60-13"
Weight	308 lbs
Wheel Base	61"
Colors	Black, Charcoal, Metallic Green, Metallic Red, Pearl White, Slate Blue
MSRP	$2,495

Retro 50, 150

	50cc	*150cc*
Engine	49.5cc four-stroke, air cooled	SYM 150cc ceramic cylinder, four-stroke air cooled, Keihin carb
Brakes Front/Rear	Disc/drum	Disc/drum
L×W×H	70"×27"×44"	70"×27"×44"
Fuel Capacity	2 gallon	2 gallon
Max Power	3.5 HP	9.8 HP
Seat Height	29"	29"
Start	Electric/kick	Electric/kick
Suspension	Front dual shock, rear mono shock	Front and rear dual shock
Tires Front/Rear	3.5×10"/3.5×10"	3.5×10"/3.5×10"
Weight	198 lbs	209 lbs
Wheel Base	50"	50"
Colors	Orange, Purple, Red, Baby Blue, Creme, Pink	Orange, Purple, Red, Baby Blue, Creme, Pink
MSRP	$1,595	$2,195

Tracer 150, 250

	150cc	*250cc*
Engine	SYM 150cc ceramic cylinder, four-stroke air	200cc liquid cooled four-stroke cooled Keihin carb
Brakes Front/Rear	Disc/disc	Disc/disc
Fuel Efficiency	75-80 mpg	75-80 mpg
Fuel Capacity	2 gallon	2 gallon
Gauges	Fuel Gauge, Odometer, Speedometer, LED Indicator Lights	Fuel Gauge, Odometer, Speedometer, LED Indicator Lights
Maximum Load	330 lbs	380 lbs
Max Power	9.8 HP	17 HP
Seat Height	29"	29"

continues

Diamo (www.DiamoUSA.com)   (continued)

Tracer 150, 250

Start	Electric/kick	Electric/kick
Suspension	Front dual shock, rear mono shock	Front and rear dual shock
Tires Front/Rear	130/60-13"/130/60-13"	130/60-13"/130/60-13"
Weight	242 lbs	262 lbs
Wheel Base	53"	53"
Colors	Blue/Silver, Blue/Yellow, Green/Silver, Orange/ Black/Silver, Purple/ Silver, Red/Silver, Silver/Black, White/ Black, Yellow/Black	Blue/Yellow, Orange/Black/ Silver, Purple/ Silver, Silver/ Black, Red/Silver
MSRP	$2,395	$3,495

Turista 260

Engine	258cc SOHC single-cylinder, four-stroke, liquid cooled
Brakes Front/Rear	Disc/disc
L×W×H	84"×29"×53"
Fuel Efficiency	60-70 mpg
Fuel Capacity	2.9 gallon
Gauges	Fuel Gauge, LED Indicator Lights, Odometer, Speedometer
Max Power	18.4 hp
Seat Height	29.7"
Suspension	Front dual shock, rear mono shock
Tires Front/Rear	110/90-12"/110/90-12"
Transmission	Automatic
Weight	370 lbs
Wheel Base	61"
Features	CDI Ignition, Rear Carrier, Under Seat, Storage Compartment, Side Mirrors
Colors	Blue, Red, Silver, Silver/Black, Silver/Blue, Silver/Red
MSRP	$3,995

Velux 150, 200

	150cc	*200cc*
Engine	SYM 150cc ceramic cylinder, four-stroke air	200cc liquid-cooled, four-stroke cooled Keihin carb
Brakes Front/Rear	Disc/disc	Disc/disc
Dimensions	80"×26"×59"	80"×26"×59"
Fuel Efficiency	75-80 mpg	75-80 mpg
Fuel Capacity	2 gallon	2 gallon
Gauges	Fuel Gauge, Odometer, Speedometer, LED Indicator Lights	Fuel Gauge, Odometer, Speedometer, LED Indicator Lights
Max Power	9.8 HP	17 HP
Seat Height	29"	29"
Suspension	Front dual shock, rear mono shock	Front and rear dual shock
Tires Front/Rear	130/60-13"/130/60-13"	130/60-13"/130/60-13"
Transmission	CVT automatic	CVT automatic
Weight	369 lbs	379 lbs
Wheel Base	57"	57"
Features	CDI Ignition, Front Glove Box Compartment, Radio/CD/MP3 Player, Rear Carrier	CDI Ignition, Front Glove Box Compartment, Radio/CD/MP3 Player, Rear Carrier
Colors	Black, Green/Blue, Metallic Red, Pearl White, Red/Black, Silver, Slate Blue, Yellow/Black	Black, Metallic Green, Metallic Red, Silver, Pearl White, Slate Blue
MSRP	$3,995	$4,495

Eton (www.EtonAmerica.com)

Beamer II

Engine Type	Two-stroke, oil-injected, single-cylinder
Displacement	49.3cc

continues

Eton (www.EtonAmerica.com)   (continued)

Beamer II

Bore/Stroke	40 mm×39.2 mm
Cooling System	Air
Gearbox	CVT
Chassis	72" l×25.5" w×43" h
Front Suspension	Telescopic forks
Rear Suspension	Swing arm with shock
Brake Front/Rear	155 mm Disc/drum
Tires F/R	120/90-10"/130/90-10 tubeless
Seat Height	30"
Wheelbase	50"
Fuel Capacity	1.4 gallons
Weight	180 lbs
Available Colors	Black, Red, Yellow
Features	Underseat storage, pillion with passenger pegs, rear rack, locking gas cap
Warranty	6 months
MSRP	$1,599

Matrix

Engine Type	Two-stroke, oil-injected, single-cylinder
Displacement	49.3cc
Bore × Stroke	40 mm×39.2 mm
Cooling System	Air
Gearbox	CVT
Chassis	72" l×25.5" w×43" h
Front Suspension	Telescoping forks
Rear Suspension	Swing arm with shock
Brakes Front/Rear	155 mm disc/drum
Tires Front/Rear	120/90-10" (tubeless)/130/90-10" (tubeless)
Seat Height	30"
Wheelbase	50"
Fuel Capacity	1.4 gallons
Weight	180 lbs
Available Colors	Black, Red, Yellow
Features	Luggage box, Pro-Flow exhaust, two-tone seat, black powder coat wheels and forks

Matrix

Warranty	6 months
MSRP	$1,799

Genuine (www.GenuineScooters.com)

Black Cat

Engine	50cc two-stroke, air cooled
Transmission	Automatic (CVT)
Colors	Yellow/Black, Red/Black
Suspension	Telescopic front fork, adjustable rear
Tires Front/Rear	120/70-12"/130/70-12"
Brakes Front/Rear	Disc/drum
Warranty	2-year/unlimited mile
MSRP	$2,099

Buddy

	50cc	*125cc*
Engine	50cc two-stroke, air cooled	125cc four-stroke, air cooled
Transmission	Automatic (CVT)	Automatic (CVT)
Colors	Charcoal, Metallic Blue, Pink	Charcoal, Metallic Blue, Pink
Tire Size	90/90 -10"	90/90 -10"
Brakes Front/Rear	Disc/drum	Disc/drum
Warranty	2-year/unlimited mile	2-year/unlimited mile
MSRP	$1,899	$2,499

Stella

Engine	150cc two-stroke, air cooled
Transmission	Manual 4-speed hand-shift
Colors	Red, Black, Orange, Mint, Blue, Pink, White

continues

Genuine (www.GenuineScooters.com)   (continued)

Stella

Accessories	Matching metal sidecars, stereo system, full chrome packages, covers and more
Chassis	Pressed-steel monocoque
Tire Size	3.5"×10" (spare included)
Braking	Front disc, rear drum
Warranty	1-year/5,000 mile
MSRP	$2,999

Honda (Powersports.Honda.com)

Big Ruckus

Engine Type	249cc liquid cooled single-cylinder four-stroke
Bore × Stroke	72.7 mm×60 mm
Compression Ratio	10.5:1
Valve Train	SOHC; two valves per cylinder
Carburetion:	30 mm CV with Auto-Enricher
Transmission	Automatic V-Matic belt drive
Suspension Front	33mm Hydraulic Fork; 3.9" travel
Suspension Rear	Single-side swing arm with dual hydraulic shocks with seven-position spring preload adjustability; 4.7" travel
Brakes Front/Rear	Single 240 mm disc w/CBS three-piston caliper/160 mm drum
Tires Front/Rear	110/90-12"/130/70-12"
Wheelbase	57.3"
Seat Height	28.2-28.7"
Dry Weight	362 lbs
Fuel Capacity	3.2 gallons
Color	Metallic Silver
MSRP	$5,499

Elite

Engine Type	80cc air cooled, single-cylinder, four-stroke
Carburetion	16 mm CV with automatic choke
Transmission	Automatic variable-ratio

Elite

Suspension Front	Bottom link; 3.0" travel
Suspension Rear	Unit swing arm; 3.1" travel
Brakes Front/Rear	Drum/drum
Tires Front/Rear	3.50×10"/3.50×10"
Wheelbase	46.1"
Seat Height	29.7"
Dry Weight	172 lbs
Capacity	1.3 gallons
Colors	Pearl/Blue/Red
MSRP	$2,349

Helix

Engine Type	244cc liquid cooled single-cylinder four-stroke
Carburetion	30mm CV with automatic choke
Transmission	Automatic V-Matic
Suspension Front	Bottom link; 3.2" travel
Suspension Rear	Swing arm with dual hydraulic shocks; 3.9" travel
Brakes Front/Rear	Single disc/drum
Tires Front/Rear	110/100-12"/120/90-10"
Wheelbase	63.8"
Seat Height	26.2"
Dry Weight	349.4 lbs
Fuel Capacity	3.2 gallons
Color	Red
MSRP	$5,299

Metropolitan II

	CHF50	CHF50/CHF50P
Engine Type	49cc liquid cooled single-cylinder four-stroke	49cc liquid cooled single-cylinder four-stroke
Carburetion	18 mm CV w/automatic choke	15 mm CV w/automatic choke
Transmission	Automatic V-Matic belt drive	Automatic V-Matic belt drive

continues

Honda (Powersports.Honda.com)   (continued)

Metropolitan II

Suspension Front	Twin-downtube fork; 1.9" travel	Twin-downtube fork; 1.9" travel
Suspension Rear	Single shock; 2.6" travel	Single shock; 2.6" travel
Brakes F/R	Drum/drum with CBS	Drum/drum with CBS
Tires F/R	90/90-10"/90/90-10"	90/90-10"/90/90-10"
Wheelbase	46.9"	46.9"
Seat Height	28.3"	28.0"
Dry Weight	163 lbs	157 lbs
Fuel Capacity	1.32 gallons	1.3 gallons
Colors	Peach Hibiscus, Red Kanji, Blue Ice, Salsa, Denim	Salsa, Denim, Solar, Blue Hibiscus, Checkers, Kanji, Orange Ice, Kiwi
MSRP	$1,849	$1,849

Reflex

Model	NSS250A (with ABS)/NSS250, NSS250AS (Sport with ABS)/NSS250S (Sport) Reflex Sport edition includes short sport-style Windshield, Chrome Grabrail with Integrated Backrest, one-piece Chrome Handlebar and Cover, Chrome Sidestand and Handlebar Caps
Engine Type	249cc liquid cooled single-cylinder four-stroke
Bore × Stroke	72.7 mm×60 mm
Compression Ratio	10.5:1
Valve Train	SOHC; two valves per cylinder
Carburetion	30 mm CV with Auto-Enricher
Transmission	Automatic V-Matic belt drive
Suspension Front	33 mm hydraulic fork; 3.9" travel
Suspension Rear	Single-side swing arm with dual hydraulic shocks with seven-position spring preload adjustability; 4.7" travel
Brakes Front	Single 240 mm disc with CBS three-piston caliper
Brakes Rear	Single 220 mm disc with CBS single-piston caliper NSS250A/NSS250AS: optional ABS

Reflex

Tires Front/Rear	110/90-13"/130/70-12"
Wheelbase	60.8"
Seat Height	28.3"
Dry Weight	NSS250A: 379 lbs, NSS250: 375 lbs, NSS250AS: 379 lbs, NSS250S: 373 lbs
Fuel Capacity	3.2 gallons
Colors	NSS250A/NSS250: Candy Blue, NSS250AS/NSS250S: Yellow
MSRP	$5,499, w/ABS $5,999/Sport: 5,499, w/ABS $5,999

Ruckus

Engine Type	49cc liquid cooled single-cylinder four-stroke
Carburetion	15mm CV with automatic choke
Transmission	Automatic V-Matic belt drive
Suspension Front	Twin-downtube fork; 2.2" travel
Suspension Rear	Single shock; 2.6" travel
Brakes Front/Rear	Drum/drum
Tires Front/Rear	120/90-10"/130/90-10"
Wheelbase	49.8"
Seat Height	28.9"
Dry Weight	181 lbs
Fuel Capacity	1.3 gallons
Colors	White/Silver Camo
MSRP	$1,999

Silver Wing

Model	FSC600A3 (with ABS)/FSC600A
Engine Type	582cc liquid cooled four-stroke parallel-twin
Bore × Stroke	72 mm×71.5 mm
Compression Ratio	10.2:1
Valve Train	DOHC; 4-valves per cylinder
Carburetion	PGM-FI with automatic enricher circuit
Transmission	Automatic V-Matic belt drive
Suspension Front	41 mm hydraulic fork; 4.7" travel

continues

Honda (Powersports.Honda.com)   (continued)

Silver Wing

Suspension Rear	Swing arm w/dual hydraulic shocks w/five-position spring preload adjustability; 4.5" travel
Brakes Front	Single 256mm disc with CBS three-piston caliper
Brakes Rear	Single 240mm disc with CBS twin-piston caliper
	FSC600A3: optional ABS
Tires Front/Rear	120/80-14"/150/70-13"
Wheelbase	62.8"
Seat Height	29.7"
Dry Weight	FSC600A3: 511 lbs/FSC600A: 501 lbs
Fuel Capacity	4.2 gallons, including 0.9-gallon reserve
Color	Metallic Blue
MSRP	$7,949, with ABS $8,449

Kymco (www.KymcoUSA.com)

Agility

Engine	Four-stroke SOHC
Displacement	49cc
Bore × Stroke	39 mm×41.4 mm
Cooling	Forced air
Transmission	CVT automatic
Suspension Front/Rear	Telescopic forks/mono shocks
Tires Front/Rear	120/70-12"/130/70-12"
Brakes Front/Rear	Disc/drum
l×w×h	72"×27"×44.5"
Wheel Base	52"
Dry Weight	203.9 lbs
Seat Height	31"
Fuel Capacity	1.32 gallons
Estimated Mpg	87
Instrumentation	Speedometer, Odometer, and Fuel

Agility

Colors	Red, Silver, Blue
Warranty	2-year factory, CA Green Sticker compliant
MSRP	$1,599

Bet and Win 150, 250

	150cc	*250cc*
Engine	4 Stroke SOHC	4 Stroke SOHC
Displacement	152cc	249cc
Bore × Stroke	57.4 mm ×57.8 mm	72.7×60
Cooling	Liquid	Liquid
Transmission	CVT automatic	CVT automatic
Suspension F/R	Telescopic forks/ dual Shocks	Telescopic forks/dual shocks
Tires F/R	120/70-12" / 130/70-12"	120/70-12"/ 140/70-12"
Brakes F/R	Disc/disc	Disc/disc
L×W×H	76.38"×29.5"×45"	29.5"×44.9"×57"
Wheel Base	55"	57"
Dry Weight	304 lbs	348 lbs
Seat Height	31"	32"
Fuel Capacity	2.6 gallons	2.8 gallons
Estimated Mpg	84	70
Instrumentation	Speedometer, Odometer, Clock and Fuel	Speedometer, Odometer, Clock and Fuel
Colors	Wine, White, Silver	Red/Silver, Charcoal/Silver
Warranty	2-year factory CA Green Sticker compliant	2-year factory CA Green Sticker compliant
MSRP	$3,499	$4,495

Grand Vista

Engine	Four-stroke SOHC
Displacement	249cc

continues

Kymco (www.KymcoUSA.com)   (continued)

Grand Vista

Bore × Stroke	72.7 mm ×60 mm
Cooling	Liquid
Transmission	CVT automatic
Suspension F/R	Telescopic forks/adjustable shocks
Tires F/R	120/70-12"/140/70-12"
Brakes F/R	Disc/disc
L×W×H	81.1"×30.3"×53.3"
Wheel Base	56.4"
Dry Weight	359 lbs
Seat Height	30.3"
Fuel Capacity	2.4 gallons
Estimated Mpg	61
Instrumentation	Speedometer, Tachometer, Odometer, Tripmeter Clock, Fuel, and Temp., 12V DC Adapter
Colors	White, Blue
Warranty	2-year factory CA Green Sticker compliant
MSRP	$4,399

People 50, 150

	50cc	*150cc*
Engine	Two-stroke oil-injected	Four-stroke SOHC
Displacement	49cc	152cc
Bore × Stroke	39 mm×41.4 mm	57.4 mm ×57 mm
Cooling	Forced air	Forced air
Transmission	CVT automatic	CVT automatic
Suspension Front/ Rear	Telescopic forks/ mono shocks	Telescopic forks/ dual shocks
Tires Front/Rear	80/80-16"/100/80-16"	80/80-16"/100/80-16"
Brakes Front/Rear	Disc/drum	Disc/drum
L×W×H	72.85"×27.5"×42.5"	76.75"×27"×42.5"
Wheel Base	50"	53"
Dry Weight	210.5 lbs	245 lbs
Seat Height	31"	31"
Fuel Capacity	1.53 gallons	1.8 gallons
Estimated Mpg	88	84

People 50, 150

Instrumentation	Speedometer, Odometer, Fuel, Low Oil Light	Speedometer, Odometer and Fuel
Colors	Ivory, Light Blue	Wine, White, Silver
Warranty	2-year factory CA Green Sticker compliant	2-year factory
MSRP	$2,299	$3,199

People 250

Engine	four-stroke SOHC
Displacement	249cc
Bore × Stroke	72.7 mm ×60 mm
Cooling	Liquid
Transmission	CVT automatic
Suspension F/R	Telescopic forks/dual shocks
Tires Front/Rear	110/70-16"/140/70-16"
Brakes Front/Rear	Disc/disc
L×W×H	87.4"×29.25"×45"
Wheel Base	59.6"
Dry Weight	367 lbs
Seat Height	30.9"
Fuel Capacity	2.1 gallons
Estimated Mpg	70
Instrumentation	Speedometer, Odometer, Clock and Fuel
Colors	Wine, Grey
Warranty	2-year factory CA Green Sticker compliant
MSRP	$3,999

Super 9

Engine	Two-stroke oil-injected
Displacement	49cc
Bore × Stroke	39 mm×41.4 mm
Cooling	Liquid
Transmission	CVT automatic
Suspension F/R	Telescopic forks/mono shocks
Tires F/R	120/70-12"/130/70-12"

continues

Kymco (www.KymcoUSA.com)   (continued)

Super 9

Brakes F/R	Disc/disc
L×W×H	72.85"×27.5"×46.85"
Wheel Base	51"
Dry Weight	234 lbs
Seat Height	32"
Fuel Capacity	1.8 gallons
Estimated Mpg	88
Instrumentation	Speedometer, Odometer, Fuel, and Low Oil Light
Colors	Red, Matte Black, Blue
Warranty	2-year factory
MSRP	$2,499

Vitality 50, 4T

	50	*4T*
Engine	Two-stroke, oil-injected	Four-stroke, SOHC
Displacement	49cc	49cc
Bore × Stroke	39 mm×41.4 mm	39 mm×41.4 mm
Cooling	Forced air	Forced air
Transmission	CVT automatic	CVT automatic
Suspension F/R	Telescopic forks/mono shocks	Telescopic forks/ mono shocks
Tires F/R	120/70-12"/ 130/70-12"	120/70-12"/ 130/70-12"
Brakes Front/Rear	Disc/drum	Disc/drum
L×W×H	73.6"×27.5"×44"	73.6"×27.5"×44"
Wheel Base	51"	51"
Dry Weight	213 lbs	213.8 lbs
Seat Height	32.8"	31"
Fuel Capacity	1.3 gallons	1.32 gallons
Est. Mpg	87	87
Instrumentation	Speedometer, Odometer, and Fuel	Speedometer, Fuel, and Low Oil Light
Colors	Red, Blue	Red, Blue

Vitality 50, 4T

Warranty	2-year factory	2-year factory, CA Green Sticker compliant
MSRP	$2,099	$2,199

Xciting 250

Engine	Four-stroke SOHC
Displacement	249cc
Bore × Stroke	72.7 mm×60 mm
Cooling	Liquid
Transmission	CVT automatic
Suspension F/R	Telescopic forks/adjustable shocks
Tires F/R	120/70-15"/150/70-14"
Brakes F/R	Disc/disc
L×W×H	90"×33"×58"
Wheel Base	62"
Dry Weight	407 lbs
Seat Height	30.3"
Fuel Capacity	2.8 gallons
Estimated Mpg	61
Instrumentation	Speedometer, Tachometer, Clock, Fuel and Temp., 12V DC Adapter, Odometer, Tripmeter
Colors	Orange, Blue, Charcoal
Warranty	2-year factory CA Green Sticker compliant
MSRP	$4,899

Xciting 500

Engine	Four-stroke DOHC
Displacement	460cc
Bore × Stroke	92 mm×69 mm
Cooling	Liquid
Transmission	CVT automatic
Suspension F/R	Telescopic forks/adjustable shocks
Tires F/R	120/70-15"/150/70-14"
Brakes F/R	Dual disc/disc
L×W×H	90"×33"×58"

continues

Kymco (www.KymcoUSA.com)   (continued)

Xciting 500

Wheel Base	62"
Dry Weight	473 lbs
Seat Height	30.3"
Fuel Capacity	2.8 gallons
Instrumentation	Speedometer, Tachometer, Clock, Fuel and Temp., 12V DC Adapter, Odometer, Tripmeter
Colors	Orange, Blue, Charcoal
Warranty	2-year factory
	CA Green Sticker compliant
MSRP	$5,999

ZX50

Engine	Two-stroke, oil-injected
Displacement	49cc
Bore × Stroke	39 mm ×41.4 mm
Cooling	Forced air
Drivetrain Transmission	CVT automatic
Suspension Front/Rear	Telescopic forks/mono shocks
Tires Front/Rear	110/70-12"/120/70-12"
Brakes Front/Rear	Disc/drum
L×W×H	70.5"×27"×41.5"
Wheel Base	48"
Dry Weight	192 lbs
Seat Height	31"
Fuel Capacity	1.29 gallons
Estimated Mpg	89
Instrumentation	Speedometer, Odometer, Fuel and Low Oil Light
Colors	Red/Silver, Blue/Silver
Warranty	2-year factory
MSRP	$1,799

Linhai (Sunright.net)

LH300 Aeolus

Engine Type	Four-stroke
Cylinders	1
Displacement	275
Bore × Stroke	72.5 mm×66.8 mm
Cooling System	Liquid
Gearbox	CVT
Front Brake	Disc
Rear Brake	Drum
Front Wheel/Tire	110/90-12
Rear Wheel/Tire	130/70-12
Wheelbase	1535 mm
Fuel Capacity	16 L
Weight	168 kg
Available Colors	Red, Blue, Black, Silver
Features	Sport styling/large engine/great fuel mileage
Warranty	12 months
MSRP	$3,599

Other models: PM 260, LH 150 Aeolus, LH 50 Aeolus

Modcycles (www.Modcycles.com)

Suntrike

Engine	Two-stroke, air cooled
Capacity	49.2cc
Power	4.4 HP
Lubrication System	Automatic
Transmission	CVT automatic
Electric System	12V
Suspension Front	Independent, hydraulic shock absorbers with height regulation
Suspension Rear	Hydraulic shock absorbers
Brakes Front/Rear	Disc, hydraulic/drum
Wheels	Alloy, 13", steel, 12"
Tires Front/Rear	130/60×13"/120/70×12"

continues

Modcycles (www.Modcycles.com) (continued)

Suntrike

Frame	Steel, tubular electrophoresis protected
Body	Fiberglass, painted with high gloss PU and UV resistant
Seating Capacity	2 Persons
Instruments	Speedometer, Fuel Indicator, Oil Level Alarm
Standard Equipment	12V socket for mobile phone, safety belts, can holder, luggage carrier under seats, anti-roll protector, 2 rearview mirrors
L×W×H	2.63 m×1.40 m×1.12 m
Wheel Base	1.88 m
Weight Curb/Gross	180 kg/350 kg
MSRP	$6,500

Piaggio (www.PiaggioUSA.com)

BV 250

Engine	Single-cylinder, four-stroke Piaggio QUASAR
cylinder	244cc
Bore × Stroke	2.8"×2.4" (72 mm×60 mm)
Max Power	22 hp at 8,250 rpm
Max Torque	20.2 Nm at 6,500 rpm
Fuel Capacity	Unleaded 91 min octane/2.6 gallons
Fuel Supply	Electronic injection system
Cooling	Liquid
Gears	CVT automatic ratio variator
Clutch	Dry automatic centrifugal type
Chassis	Twin cradle tubes in high tensile steel
F Suspension	Telescopic fork, 35 mm shafts, 104 mm travel
R Suspension	Dual hydraulic shock absorber, four-position spring preload, 90 mm travel
F Brake	260 mm disc, floating caliper w/2 pistons
R Brake	260 mm disc, floating caliper w/opposed pistons
F/R Tire	Tubeless 110/70, 16"/140/70, 16"
Length	83.1" (2,110 mm)
Width	29.9" (760 mm)

BV 250

Wheelbase	57.9" (1,470 mm)
Seat Height	30.9" (785 mm)
Dry Weight	328 lbs (149 kg)
Colors	Canyon Red, Graphite Black
MSRP	$4,499

BV 500

Engine	Single-cylinder, four-stroke catalytic Piaggio MASTER
cylinder	460cc
Bore × Stroke	3.6"×2.7" (92 mm×69 mm)
Max Power	29 kW at 7,500 rpm
Max Torque	43 Nm at 5,500 rpm
Fuel Capacity	Unleaded 91 min octane/3.49 gallons (13.2 liters)
Fuel Supply	Electronic injection system
Dist valves	Single overhead camshaft (SOHC) with four
Cooling	Liquid
Lubrication	Wet sump
Gears	CVT automatic ratio variator
Clutch	Centrifugal
Chassis	Double cradle in high-tensile steel tubes
F Suspension	41 mm telescopic hydraulic forks
R Suspension	Two dual-effect hydraulic dampers, four-position coil spring
F Brake	Twin stainless steel discs 260 mm with fixed twin piston calipers 32–34 mm left /right
R Brake	Stainless steel disc 240 mm w/fixed opposed pistons 34 mm
F/R Tire Tubeless	110/70, 16"/150/70, 14"
Length×Width	87.2" (2,215 mm)×30.3" (770 mm)
Wheelbase	61" (1,550 mm)
Seat Height	30.5" (775 mm)
Dry Weight	416 lbs (189 kg)
Colors	Burgundy, Black
MSRP	$6,199

continues

Piaggio (www.PiaggioUSA.com)   (continued)

Fly 150

Engine cylinder	Single-cylinder, four-stroke Piaggio LEADER 150cc
Bore × Stroke	2.5"×1.9" (62.6 mm×48.6 mm)
Max Power	8.5 kW at 7,750 rpm (11.6 bhp)
Max Torque	11.5 Nm at 6,000 rpm
Fuel Capacity	Unleaded 91 min octane/1.9 gallons
Cooling	Forced air
Gears	CVT automatic ratio variator (Twist-and-Go)
Clutch	Dry automatic centrifugal type
Chassis	Tube type
F Suspension	Telescopic hydraulic forks 32 mm
R Suspension	Hydraulic single shock absorber
F/R Brake	Disc 200 mm, floating caliper with two pistons, drum 140 mm
F/R Tire	Tubeless 120/70, 12"
L×W	73.6" (1,870 mm)×28.9" (735 mm)
Wheelbase	52.4" (1,330 mm)
Seat Height	30.9" (785 mm)
Dry Weight	247 lbs (112 kg)
Colors	Dragon Red, Marine Blue
MSRP	$3,399

Typhoon, SE

Engine cylinder	Single-cylinder, two-stroke 49cc
Bore × Stroke	1.57"×1.54"
Fuel Capacity	Unleaded 91 min octane/1.5 gallons (5.2 liters)
Cooling System	Air with forced ventilation
Lubrication	Separate with automatic mixer
Gears	CVT automatic ratio variator (Twist-and-Go) and torque server
Clutch	Automatic centrifugal type
Chassis	Welded steel tubes with pressed steel reinforcements
F Suspension	Hydraulic telescopic fork with upside-down shafts

Typhoon, SE

R Suspension	Hydraulic double effect single damper, co-axial helicoidal spring
F Brake	Hydraulic 7.5" (190 mm) stainless steel disc
R Brake	Drum 3.94" (100 mm), mechanically commanded
F/R Tire	Tubeless 120/90, 10"/tubeless 120/90, 10"
L×W	78.87"×27.56"
Wheelbase	50.39" (1,280 mm)
Seat Height	31.1" (790 mm)
Dry Weight	179 lbs (81 kg)
Colors	Black, Cosmic Blue, and Special Limited Edition Champ Car-Newman/Haas Typhoon
MSRP	$1,999, Special Edition: $2,099

X9

Engine	Single-cylinder, four-stroke, 4-valve Piaggio MASTER
cylinder	460cc
Bore × Stroke	3.6"×2.7" (92 mm×69 mm)
Max Power	29 kW at 7,500 rpm (39 bhp)
Max Torque	43 Nm at 5,500 rpm
Fuel Capacity	Unleaded 91 min octane/3.9 gallons (15 liters)
Fuel Supply	Electronic injection system
Dist	Single overhead camshaft (SOHC) with four valves
Cooling System	Liquid
Starter	Electronic with automatic choke
Gears	CVT automatic ratio variator (Twist-and-Go)
Clutch	Centrifugal
F Suspension	Telescopic hydraulic fork, stem 1.6" (41 mm), stroke 3.54" (90 mm)
R Suspension	Two dual-effect hydraulic dampers, helical springs, adjustable to four positions of pre-load, stroke 3.54" (90 mm)
F Brake	Stainless steel double discs, 10.2" (260 mm), floating "Brembo Serie Oro" caliper with twin pistons: 1.1" (28 mm), front right; 1.02" (26 mm), front left

continues

Piaggio (www.PiaggioUSA.com) (continued)

X9

R Brake	Stainless steel discs, 9.45" (240 mm); "Brembo Serie Oro" caliper 1.34" (34 mm)
F/R Tire	Tubeless 120/70, 14"/tubeless 150/70, 14"
Length/Width	83.8" (2,140 mm)/34.6" (880 mm)
Wheelbase	60.2" (1,530 mm)
Seat Height	30.7" (780 mm)
Dry Weight	454 lbs (206 kg)
Colors	Excalibur Gray, Imperial Blue
MSRP	$6,399

Schwinn (www.SchwinnScooters.com)

Campus, Hope

Engine	Four-stroke, air cooled
Displacement	49.5cc
Cylinders	1
Starter	Electric/kick
Transmission	CVT automatic
Tires Front/Rear	3.5-10"/3.5-10"
Rims	Steel
Brakes F/R	Drum/drum
Suspension F/R	Telescopic fork/damping shock
Seat Storage	0.64 cu ft
L×W×H	68.4"×24.9"×41.9"
Dry Weight	163.4 lbs
Fuel Capacity	1.45 gallons
Gas Mileage	117 mpg
Warranty	1-year parts and labor
Hope Color	Pink/White
Campus Colors	Black/White, Blue/White
MSRP	$1,499

A portion of the proceeds from the Hope model will support breast cancer awareness and research.

Collegiate

Engine	Four-stroke, air cooled
Displacement	49.5cc
Cylinders	1
Transmission	CVT automatic
Tires Front/Rear	3.5-10"/3.5-10"
Rims	Aluminum
Brakes Front/Rear	Disc/drum
Suspension F/R	Telescopic fork/damping shock
Seat Storage	0.64 cu ft
(L×W×H)	68.3"×25.4"×43.1"
Dry Weight	161.9 lbs
Fuel Capacity	1.45 gallons
Gas Mileage	117 mpg
Warranty	1-year parts and labor
Colors	Red/White, Silver/White
MSRP	$1,599

Graduate

	50cc	*150cc*
Engine	Four-stroke, air cooled	Four-stroke, air cooled
Displacement	49.5cc	150cc
Cylinders	1	1
Transmission	CVT automatic	CVT automatic
Tires Front/Rear	3.5-10"/3.5-10"	3.5-10"/3.5-10"
Brakes F/R	Disc/drum	Disc/drum
Suspension F/R	Telescopic fork/ damping shock	Telescopic fork/ damping shock
Seat Storage	0.70 cu ft	0.70 cu ft
L×W×H	71.3"×27.2"×44.5"	69.9"×26.6"×43.3"
Dry Weight	188.1 lbs	213.7 lbs
Fuel Capacity	1.32 gallons	1.59 gallons
Gas Mileage	117 mpg	87 mpg
Warranty	1-year parts and labor	1-year parts and labor

continues

Schwinn (www.SchwinnScooters.com) (continued)

Graduate

Colors	Silver, Metallic Blue	Burgundy, Charcoal
MSRP	$1,799	$1,999

Sport 50, 150

	50cc	*150cc*
Engine	Four-stroke, air cooled	Four-stroke, air cooled
Displacement	49.5cc	150cc
Cylinders	1	1
Transmission	CVT automatic	CVT automatic
Tires Front/Rear	120/70-12"/130/70-12"	110/70-12"/120/70-12"
Rims	Steel	Aluminum
Brakes F/R	Disc/drum	Disc/drum
Suspension F/R	Telescopic fork/damping	Telescopic shock fork/damping shock
Seat Storage	0.60 cu ft	0.70 cu ft
LxWxH	72.8"×26.8"×44.9"	71.6"×26.2"×44.2"
	50cc	*150cc*
Dry Weight	198 lbs	244.5 lbs
Fuel Capacity	1.05 gallons	1.72 gallons
Gas Mileage	117 mpg	87 mpg
Warranty	1-year parts and labor	1-year parts and labor
Colors	Black, Sport Red	Black, Red
MSRP	$1,699	$2,399

Suzuki (www.SuzukiCycles.com)

Burgman 400, 400S

	400	*400 Type S*
Engine	385cc, four-stroke, liquid cooled, single-cylinder, SOHC, 4-valve	385cc, four-stroke, liquid-cooled, twin-cylinder, SOHC, 4-valve

Burgman 400, 400S

Warranty	12-month unlimited mileage limited warranty	12-month unlimited mileage limited warranty
Bore × Stroke	83.0 mm ×71.2 mm	83.0 mm ×71.2 mm
Compression ratio	10.2:1	10.2:1
Fuel System	Fuel injection	Fuel injection
Lubrication	Wet sump	Wet sump
Transmission	V-belt, CVT automatic	V-belt, CVT automatic
Final Drive	Shaft	Shaft
L×W×H	89"×29.9"×54.1"	89"×29.9"×54.1"
Seat Height	27.4"	27.4"
Ground Clearance	4.9"	4.9"
Wheelbase	62.6"	62.6"
Dry Weight	405 lbs	405 lbs
Suspension Front	Telescopic, oil damped	Telescopic, oil damped
	400	*400 Type S*
Suspension Rear	Link-type, adjustable preload	Link-type, adjustable preload
Brakes Front/Rear	Single hydraulic disc/ single hydraulic disc	Single hydraulic disc/ single hydraulic disc
Tires Front/Rear	110/90-13"/130/70-13"	110/90-13"/130/70-13"
Fuel Capacity	3.4 gallon	3.4 gallon
Color	Gray	Blue
MSRP	$5,699	$5,849

Burgman 650, 650 Executive

Engine	638cc, four-stroke, liquid cooled, twin-cylinder, DOHC, 4-valve
Warranty	12-month unlimited mileage, limited warranty
Bore × Stroke	75.5 mm×71.3 mm
Compression Ratio	11.2:1
Fuel System	Fuel injection
Lubrication	Wet sump
Transmission	Electronically-controlled, CVT automatic
Final Drive	Gear
L×W×H	89.0"×31.9"×56.5"

continues

Suzuki (www.SuzukiCycles.com)   (continued)

Burgman 650, 650 Executive

Seat Height	29.5"
Ground Clearance	5.1"
Wheelbase	62.8"
Dry Weight	524 lbs
Suspension Front	Telescopic, oil damped
Suspension Rear	Twin shock, adjustable preload
Brakes Front/Rear	Dual hydraulic disc/single hydraulic disc
Tires Front/Rear	120/70-R15"/160/60-R14"
Fuel Capacity	4.0 gallon
Colors	Gray, White
MSRP	$7,799

The Burgman 650 Executive has all the features of the Burgman 650 with ABS, an electric adjustable windshield, and a passenger backrest.
MSRP	$8,799.

TGB/Cobra PowerSports (www.CobraSales.com)

Delivery 50, 150

	50cc	*150cc*
Engine	Two-stroke Performance Series™ engine	Four-stroke Performance Series™ engine
Cooling	air cooled	air cooled
Cylinder Number	1	1
Displacement	49.3cc	151.1cc
Carburetor	Mikuni 13 mm	Mikuni
Max Power	4.9 HP at 7,500 rpm	10.1 HP at 7,500 rpm
Fuel Capacity	1.8 gallons	1.8 gallons
Gear Shift	Fully CVT automatic V-belt	Fully CVT automatic V-belt
L×W×H	75"×26"×45.3"	75"×26"×45.3"
Dry Weight	231.5 lbs	301 lbs
Cargo Capacity	39.6 gallons (150 L)	39.6 gallons (150 L)
Suspension Front	Inverted hydraulic shocks	Inverted hydraulic shocks

Delivery 50, 150

Suspension Rear	Mono coil over shock	Mono coil over shock
Brake F/R	Hydraulic 220mm disc, sealed drum	Hydraulic 220mm disc, sealed drum
Tires Front/Rear	14"/13"	13"/13"
MSRP	$2,299	$2,999

Key West

Engine	49cc, two-stroke
Cooling	Forced air
Fuel Consumption	70+ mpg
Carburetor	Mikuni 13 mm
Max Power	4.9 HP/7,500 rpm
Fuel Capacity	1.3 gallons
Gear Shift	Fully automatic CVT V-belt drive
L×W×H	66.7"×25.5"×42.3"
Dry Weight	178.5 lbs
Suspension	Adventure series sport tuned
Brake Front	Adventure Series 190 mm disc
Brake Rear	Drum
Tires Front/Rear	120/90-10"/120/90-10"
Colors	Retro Blue, Red, Metallic Black, Yellow
Warranty	2-year unlimited mileage for parts and labor.
MSRP	$1,699

R5, R9

	R5 49cc	*R9 151cc*
Engine	Two-stroke 2006 EPA Certified	Four-stroke 2006 EPA Certified Performance Series™
Cooling	Air cooled	Air cooled
Cylinder Number	1	1
Piston Displacement	49.3cc	151.1cc
Carburetor	Mikuni 13 mm	Mikuni
Max Power	4.4 HP at 7,500 rpm	10.1 HP at 7,500 rpm
Fuel Capacity	1.3 gallons	1.3 gallons

continues

TGB/Cobra PowerSports (www.CobraSales.com) (continued)

R5, R9

Gear Shift	Fully CVT automatic V-belt	Fully automatic CVT V-belt
Total Length	72"	73.2"
Total Width	26"	26"
Total Height	46"	46"
Dry Weight	202 lbs	268.9 lbs
Brake Front	Hydraulic 190mm disc	Hydraulic 190mm disc
Brake Rear	Sealed drum	Sealed drum
Tires Front/Rear	120/70-12"/120/70-12"	130/60-13"/130/60-13"
MSRP	$1,899	$2,599

R50X

Engine	2006 EPA Certificated, TGB Performance Series™ engine
Cooling	Two-stroke forced air cooling
Fuel Consumption	60+ mpg
cylinder Number	1
Piston Displacement	49.3cc
Carburetor	Mikuni 13 mm
Fuel Capacity	1.8 gallons
Gear Shift	Fully automatic CVT V-belt
Total Length	72"
Total Width	25"
Total Height	44"
Dry Weight	209 lbs
Front Suspension	Inverted hydraulic shocks
Rear Suspension	Racing tuned
Mono Coil Over Shock	Racing tuned
Brake Front	Hydraulic 220 mm disc
Brake Rear	Hydraulic 190 mm disc
Tires Front/Rear	130/60-13"/130/60-13"
MSRP	$2,099

TNG (www.TNGScooters.com)

Baja

Engine	Four-stroke, single-cylinder
Displacement	150cc
Cooling System	Air
Transmission	CVT—Twist-and-Go
Suspension F/R	Telescopic/hydraulic Shock
Brakes Front/Rear	Disc/drum
Tires Front/Rear	130/60×13"/130/60×13"
Seat Height	31"
Wheel Base	50"
Fuel Capacity	1.5 gallons
Weight	250 lbs
Colors	Flat Black
Warranty	Basic: 1-year parts and labor Engine: 2-years parts and labor
MSRP	$2,695

DR 150

Engine	Four-stroke single-cylinder
Displacement	150cc
Cooling System	Air
Transmission	CVT—Twist-and-Go
Suspension F/R	Telescopic/hydraulic shock
Brakes F/R	Disc/drum
Tires F/R	130/60×13"/130/60×13"
Seat Height	30"
Fuel Capacity	1.6 gallons
Weight	253 lbs
Colors	Blue/Silver, Red/Silver, Black/Silver
Warranty	Basic: 1-year parts and labor Engine: 2-years parts and labor
MSRP	$2,395

Low Boy

Engine	Four-stroke, single-cylinder
Displacement	150cc

continues

TNG (www.TNGScooters.com) (continued)

Low Boy

Cooling System	Air
Transmission	CVT—Twist-and-Go
Suspension F/R	Telescopic/hydraulic shock
Brakes Front/Rear	Disc/drum
Tires Front/Rear	3.5×10"/3.5×10"
Seat Height	28.5"
Fuel Capacity	1.6 gallons
Weight	225 lbs
Colors	Black, Silver, Rust
Warranty	Basic: 1-year parts and labor
	Engine: 2-years parts and labor
MSRP	$2,395

Milano 50, 150

	50cc	150cc
Engine	Four-stroke, single-cylinder	Four-stroke, single-cylinder
Displacement	49cc	150cc
Cooling System	Air	Air
Transmission	CVT—Twist-and-Go	CVT—Twist-and-Go
Suspension F/R	Telescopic/hydraulic shock	Telescopic/hydraulic shock
Brakes Front/Rear	Disc/drum	Disc/drum
Tires Front/Rear	3.5×10"/3.5×10"	3.5×10"/3.5×10"
Seat Height	31"	31"
Wheel Base	50"	50"
Fuel Capacity	1.5 gallons	1.5 gallons
Weight	212 lbs	249 lbs
Colors	Pearl Green, Yellow, Charcoal	Pearl Green, Yellow, Charcoal
Warranty	Basic: 1-year parts and labor	Basic: 1-year parts and labor
	Engine: 2-years parts and labor	Engine: 2-years parts and labor
MSRP	$1,795	$2,195

Venice

Engine	Four-stroke, single-cylinder
Displacement	49cc
Cooling System	Air
Transmission	CVT—Twist-and-Go
Suspension F/R	Telescopic/hydraulic shock
Brakes Front/Rear	Disc/drum
Tires Front/Rear	3.5×10"/3.5×10"
Seat Height	29"
Wheel Base	48"
Fuel Capacity	1.5 gallons
Weight	165 lbs
Colors	Black, Blue, Green
Warranty	Basic: 1-year parts and labor
	Engine: 2-years parts and labor
MSRP	$1,595

Verona

Engine	Four-stroke, single-cylinder
Displacement	150cc
Cooling System	Water
Transmission	CVT—Twist-and-Go
Suspension F/R	Telescopic/adjustable hydraulic shock
Brakes F/R	Disc/disc
Tires Front/Rear	100/80×16"/100/80×16"
Seat Height	31"
Wheel Base	53"
Fuel Capacity	1.8 gallons
Weight	278 lbs
Colors	Red, Black
Warranty	Basic: 1-year parts and labor
	Engine: 2-years parts and labor
MSRP	$2,895

continues

United Motors (www.UMAmerica.com)

Matrix 150

Engine	149cc, four-stroke, single cylinder
Bore × Stroke	57.4 mm×57.8 mm
Compression Ratio	9.2 to 1
Cooling	Air
Transmission	1-Speed automatic
Final Drive	V-belt
Starting System	Electric/kick
Suspension F/R	Telescopic fork/hydraulic dual shocks
Brakes Front/Rear	ABD Type Disc 8.50 in/drum
Tires Front/Rear	130/60-13"/130/60-13"
L×W×H	74"×28"×50"
Seat Height	30"
Wheel Base	54"
Fuel Capacity	1.7 gallons
Dry Weight	229 lbs
Colors	Blue, Red, Yellow, Black, Orange, Green
MSRP	$1,999

Power Max 150

Engine	149cc, four-stroke, single cylinder
Bore × Stroke	57.4 mm×57.8 mm
Compression Ratio	9.2 to 1
Cooling	Air
Transmission	1-speed automatic
Final Drive	V-belt
Starting System	Electric/kick
Suspension F/R	Telescopic fork/mono shock
Brakes F/R	ABD type disc 8.50 in/drum
Tires F/R	120/70-12"/120/70-12"
L×W×H	71"×27"×47"
Seat Height	30"
Wheel Base	51"
Fuel Capacity	1.5 gallons
Dry Weight	223 lbs
Colors	Black, Blue, Red, Orange
MSRP	$1,699

X-Peed 50

Engine	49cc, two-stroke, single cylinder
Bore × Stroke	41.0 mm×37.4 mm
Compression Ratio	7.2 to 1
Cooling	Air
Transmission	1 speed auto
Final Drive	V-belt
Starting System	Electric/kick
Suspension F/R	Telescopic fork/mono shock
Brakes Front/Rear	Hydraulic disc 6.40 in/drum
Tires Front/Rear	110/70-12"/120/70-12"
L×W×H	72"×25"×44"
Seat Height	31"
Wheel Base	56"
Fuel Capacity	1.3 gallons
Dry Weight	209 lbs
Colors	Red, Black
MSRP	$1,599

Vento (www.Vento.com)

Triton

Engine	Two-stroke, air cooled
Cylinders	1
Displacement	49cc
Running Diameter	40 mm×39.2 mm
Max Power	4.9 HP/7000 rpm (unrestricted), 1.9HP (with restrictor)
Maximum Torque	6.8 lbs-ft at 6500 rpm
Starting System	Electric
Fuel Capacity	1.4 gallon
Transmission	CVT automatic
Dimensions	74.4"×27.2"×50.8"
Seat Height	29.1"
Dry Weight	207 lbs
Suspension	Hydraulic sport-tuned

continues

Vento (www.Vento.com)   (continued)

Triton

Brakes Front/Rear	ABS disc/drum
Tires Front/Rear	120/70-12"/130/70-12"
Features	Indigo—Glow® back light instrument panel, digital clock, ultra comfort handlebar and handgrips, Protech® anti-theft security system, wireless remote control ignition, silktouch polyurethane seat
MSRP	$1,799

Phantera

Engine	Four-stroke, air cooled
Displacement	150cc
Running Diameter	57.4 mm×57.8 mm
Max Power	9.4 HP/7600 rpm
Maximum Torque	6.3 lbs-ft at 5100 rpm
Fuel Capacity	1.4 gallon
Transmission	CVT automatic
L×W×H	74.4"×27.2"×50.8"
Seat Height	34.8"
Dry Weight	229 lbs
Suspension	Hydraulic (sport-tuned)
Brakes Front/Rear	ABS disc/drum
Tires Front/Rear	130/60-13"/130/60-13"
Rims	Lightweight cast-aluminum 13" 3-spoke
Exhaust System	Silverstone® high-performance
Features	Carbon fiber finish, Indigo—Glow® electronic, instrumental panel, digital clock, ultra comfort handlebar and handgrips, Protech® anti-theft security system
MSRP	$2,699

Phantom

Engine	Four-stroke, air cooled
Cylinders	1
Displacement	150cc
Max Power	9.38 HP/7500 rpm

Phantom

Fuel Capacity	1.4 gallon
Transmission	CVT automatic
L×W×H	74.4"×27.4"×45"
Seat Height	32"
Dry Weight	220 lbs
Suspension	Hydraulic (sport-tuned)
Brakes Front/Rear	Hydraulic ABS disc/drum
Tires Front/Rear	130/60-13"/130/60-13"
Rims	Sport Aluminum
Colors	Red, Blue, Green, Orange
Exhaust System	Silverstone® high-performance
Features	Indigo—Glow® electronic, instrumental panel
MSRP	$2,399

Vespa (www.VespaUSA.com)

GT 200 (Granturismo)

Type	Piaggio LEADER single-cylinder, four-stroke
Cylinder Capacity	198cc
Bore × Stroke	2.8"×1.9"
Max Power at Shaft	14.7 kW at 9,000 rpm (20 CV)
Max Torque	16.5 Nm at 6,750 rpm
Fuel Capacity	2.64 gallons
Cooling System	Liquid
Gears	Automatic Twist-and-Go transmission
F Suspension	Single-arm with hydraulic shock absorber
R Suspension	Engine swing arm with two hydraulic shock absorbers
Chassis	Load-bearing steel
Tires Front/Rear	120/70-12"/130/70-12"
Length/Width	76.4"×29.7"
Wheelbase	54.9" (1,395 mm)
Seat Height	31.1" (790 mm)
Dry Weight	304 lbs

continues

Vespa (www.VespaUSA.com)   (continued)

GT 200 (Granturismo)

Colors	Smoky Gray, Excalibur Gray, Graphite Black, Vintage Green
MSRP	$5,199

GTS 250

Type	Piaggio QUASAR single-cylinder, four-stroke
Cylinder Capacity	244cc
Max Power at Shaft	16.2 kW at 8,250 rpm (22 CV)
Max Torque	20.2 Nm at 6,500 rpm
Fuel Capacity	2.4 gallons
Cooling System	Liquid
Gears	Automatic Twist-and-Go transmission
Chassis	Load-bearing steel
Tires Front/Rear	120/70-12"/130/70-12"
Length/Width	76.4"×29.7"
Dry Weight	326 lbs
Colors	Green, Black, Silver
MSRP	$5,799

LX 50, 150

	50	*150*
Type	Single-cylinder, four-stroke catalytic high-performance	Single-cylinder, four-stroke catalytic leader
Cylinder Capacity	49.4cc	150cc
Max Power at Shaft	3.1 kW at 8,750 rpm	8.7 kW at 7,750 rpm (11.7 CV)
Max Torque	3.5 Nm at 6,500 rpm	11.5 Nm at 6,000 rpm
Fuel Capacity	2.3 gallons	2.3 gallons
Cooling System	Ram air with sound proof cover	Ram air with sound proof cover
Gears	Automatic Twist-and-Go transmission	Automatic Twist-and-Go transmission
Chassis	Load-bearing steel	Load-bearing steel
Tires Front/Rear	110/70-11"/120/70-10"	110/70-11"/120/70-10"

LX 50, 150

Length/Width	69.1"/29.1"	69.1"/29.1"
Dry Weight	225 lbs	243 lbs
Colors	Red, Blue, Silver, Black, Burgandy	Red, Blue, Silver, Black, Burgandy
MSRP	$3,199	$4,199

PX 150

Type	Single-cylinder, two-stroke
Cylinder Capacity	151cc
Max Power at Shaft	6.6 kW at 5,700 rpm
Max Torque	11.9 Nm at 4,000 rpm
Fuel Capacity	2.1 gallons
Cooling System	Forced air
Gears	Manual, 4-speed
Chassis	Load-bearing steel
Tires Front/Rear	3.5-10"/3.5-10"
Length/Width	71.3"×29.1"
Dry Weight	23 lbs
Colors	Green, Red, Silver
MSRP	$4,199

Yamaha (www.Yamaha-Motor.com)

Majesty

Engine	400cc, liquid-cooled, DOHC, 4-valve, four-stroke single
Bore × Stroke	83 mm ×73 mm
Compression Ratio	10.6:1
Transmission	centrifugal clutch
Final Drive	Double-cog V-belt (automatic)
Suspension/Front	41 mm telescopic fork
Suspension/Rear	Twin shocks
Brakes/Front	267 mm Disc
Brakes/Rear	267 mm Disc
Tires/Front	120/80-14
Tires/Rear	150/70-13

continues

Yamaha (www.Yamaha-Motor.com)   (continued)

Majesty

L×W×H	87.8"×30.7"×54.3"
Seat Height	29.5"
Wheelbase	61.6"
Dry Weight	436 lbs
Fuel Capacity	3.7 gallons
Colors	Candy Red, Liquid Silver
Warranty	1-year (limited factory warranty)
MSRP	$5,799

Morphous

Engine	249cc, liquid-cooled, four-stroke, DOHC, 4-valve
Bore × Stroke	66.0 mm×73.0 mm
Compression Ratio	10.8:1
Carburetion	FI
Transmission	V-belt automatic
Final Drive	Belt
Suspension/Front	Telescopic fork
Suspension/Rear	Unit swing
Brakes/Front	Hydraulic single disc
Brakes/Rear	Hydraulic single disc
Tires/Front	120/70-13M/C 53P
Tires/Rear	130/70-13M/C 63P
L×W×H	93.3"×32.5"×41.3"
Seat Height	25.8"
Wheelbase	63.6"
Ground Clearance	4.1"
Dry Weight	408 lbs
Fuel Capacity	3.7 gallons
Colors	Raven, Galaxy Blue
MSRP	$5,199

Vino Classic

Engine	49cc, liquid-cooled, four-stroke single
Bore × Stroke	N/A
Compression Ratio	N/A

Vino Classic

Carburetion	14 mm Teikei
Transmission	V-belt automatic
Suspension/Front	Telescopic fork; 2.1" travel
Suspension/Rear	Single shock; 1.9" travel
Brakes/Front	110 mm drum
Brakes/Rear	110 mm drum
Tires/Front	80/90-10
Tires/Rear	80/90-10
Wheelbase	45.3"
Dry Weight	155 lbs
Fuel Capacity	1.6 gallons
Warranty	1-year (limited gactory warranty)
Colors	Raven, Liquid Silver, Raspberry Metallic
MSRP	$1,849

Vino 125

Type	124cc, air-cooled, SOHC, 2-valve, four-stroke single
Bore × Stroke	51.5 mm ×60 mm
Compression Ratio	9.8:1
Carburetion	26 mm Mikuni
Transmission	V-belt automatic
Suspension/Front	Telescopic fork; 3.15" travel
Suspension/Rear	Single shock; 2.56" travel
Brakes/Front	180 mm single disc, single piston
Brakes/Rear	110 mm drum
Tires/Front	3.50-10 51J
Tires/Rear	3.50-10 51J
Length	69.1"
Width	27.5"
Height	41.8"
Seat Height	29.9"
Wheelbase	48.4"
Dry Weight	229 lbs
Fuel Capacity	1.2 gallons
Warranty	1-year (limited factory warranty)

continues

Yamaha (www.Yamaha-Motor.com) (continued)

Vino 125

Colors	Team Yamaha Blue, Silver
MSRP	$2,499

Appendix B

Resources

Print Publications

This is by no means an unabridged or comprehensive list of every book on scooters. There are several general books on scooters as a whole, most of which have fantastic photos. Some of these books are referential in nature while others are travel novels. A few books also discuss scooter subcultures.

Also included on this list are books about better riding. Though they are for motorcycles, the techniques and information are applicable to scooters as well.

Also listed are a few repair manuals that are quite notable. There are many more manuals for vintage scooters that can be found through scooter shops, or online through scooter-parts vendors or through book sellers.

Books

Beagle, Peter S. *I See by My Outfit: Cross Country by Scooter, an Adventure*. North Pomfret, VT: Trafalgar Square Publishing, 2002

Bigongiali, Athos. *Vespa: Italian Style for the World*. Florence, Italy: Piaggio and C.s.p.a., 2003.

Brown, Gareth. *Scooter Boys.* Chicago: Olmstead Press, 2001.

Cox, Nigel. *Lambretta Innocenti: An Illustrated History.* Sparkford, UK: Haynes Publishing, 2002.

Dregni, Eric and Michael. *The Scooter Bible.* Center Conway, NH: Whitehorse Press, 2005.

Fort, Matthew. *Eating up Italy: Voyages on a Vespa.* London: HarperPerennial, 2005.

Goyard, Jean and Bernard Soler-Thebes. *The A-Z of Scooters: The Illustrated Guide to All Makes and Models.* Sparkford, UK: Haynes Publishing, 2007.

Hough, David L. *Proficient Motorcycling: The Ultimate Guide to Riding Well.* Irvine, CA: BowTie Press, 2000.

Hough, David. *More Proficient Motorcycling: Mastering the Ride.* Irvine, CA: BowTie Press, 2003.

LaReau, Kara (author) and Jenna (illustrator). *Rocko and Spanky Go to a Party.* New York: Harcourt Children's Books, 2004.

Moore, Peter. *Vroom With a View.* London: Centro Books, 2006.

Motorcycle Safety Foundation. *The Motorcycle Safety Foundation's Guide to Motorcycling Excellence: Skills, Knowledge, and Strategies for Riding Right.* Center Conway, NH: Whitehorse Press, 2005.

Rawlings, Terry. *Mod a Very British Phenomenon: Clean Living Under Difficult Circumstances.* London: Omnibus Press, 2000.

Shattuck, Colin. *Scooters: Red Eyes, White Walls, and Blue Smoke.* Denver: Speck Press, 2005.

Manuals

Mather, Phil. *Twist and Go Scooters 50 to 250cc.* Sparkford, UK: Haynes Publications, 2004.

How to Restore and Maintain Your Vespa Motorscooter. St. Paul, MN: Motorbooks, 1999.

Haynes Vespa P/Px 125, 150 & 200 Scooters. Sparkford, UK: Haynes
Publications, 2003.

Tessera, Vittorio. *Lambretta Restoration Guide.* Vimodrone, Italy: Giorgio
Nada Editore, 2005.

Online Resources

These are a few highlights of the scooter-related online resources currently available. There are many others, though all of these sites are
great places to start.

Bulletin Board Sites

Scooter BBS
www.scooterbbs.com
Since 1996, it's the granddaddy of scooter forums.

Stella Speed
www.stellaspeed.com
A message board specifically for the Genuine Stella and other metal-
body, manual-shift scooters.

Modern Vespa
www.modernvespa.com
Message board for discussing automatic Vespa and Piaggio scooters.

Modern Buddy
www.modernbuddy.com
The community for the new, automatic scooters from the Genuine
Scooter Company like the Buddy and Blur.

Online Groups

Yahoo! Groups is one place where scooter discussion has really taken
off. There are brand- and model-specific discussion groups, as well as a
few generalized groups. TwistnGoScoot is a large group focused on all
automatic scooters.

Other message-group services have popped up and people are using those as well for scooter-related areas. Your best bet is to thoroughly search them all for the information you're interested in.

Organizations

The following organizations advocate on behalf of riders and scooterists.

NMSDA

The National Motor Scooter Dealer's Association (NMSDA) is an organization that certifies scooter dealerships who meet specific criteria, and agree to a code of conduct. The association also partners with groups of individuals, shops, and manufacturers to promote scooter-friendly policy at local levels of government. Presently all NSMDA contact is through Scooter World Kansas City.

Mike Levitt, Founder
Phone: 913-649-4900

NMSDA c/o Scooter World KC
7325 W. 79th St.
Overland Park, KS 66204

MSF

The Motorcycle Safety Foundation develops riding education and training programs to improve rider safety. To find classes in your area, check their website or call the 800 number provided.

1-800-446-9227
www.msf-usa.org

Appendix C

Glossary

ABS—Anti-lock brake system. ABS promises shorter braking times and safer braking. It should prevent lock-up in most situations, which should keep the vehicle upright and stable. ABS on a motorcycle does little to help with cornering while braking. Braking in a turn will still destabilize a scooter or motorcycle.

ABS plastic   Plastic made of Acrylonitrile Butadiene Styrene, a rigid thermoplastic material with high-impact strength.

aftermarket   Parts produced and sold by someone other than the manufacturer.

air cooled   A method for regulating engine temperature on scooters. Usually a fan is employed to force air over metal fins to conduct excess heat away from the engine.

battery tender   A type of battery charger to keep batteries ready to go.

blind spot   The area in the next lane toward the back of a car where a driver cannot see you either directly or with peripheral vision.

buffeting   A vibration or shaking due to an aerodynamic wake. It can often feel like gusty winds, while the wind is actually consistent.

cager A motorcycle and scooter slang term for those driving cars, in reference to the bodywork that surrounds them like a cage. Though usually it's tongue in cheek, it can be a mildly derogatory term.

CARB California Air Resource Board.

carburetor A device that mixes air and fuel at the proper ratio. It also controls the engine speed.

CDI Capacitive Discharge Ignition is common in the majority of new scooters. It is an electronic system that fires the spark plug to ignite fuel and air in the engine.

CE armor Three levels of certification are offered for armor sold on the European market. Level three is the most protective, and is required in racing. Level one is for slower riding and can absorb half the impact of level three.

chain drive Propels a scooter in the same fashion as a bicycle chain and sprockets.

crash bars Also known as highway bars, these are additional chrome bars, used to protect a scooter's body panels should it fall over.

cruising speed A speed where you still have power for accelerating, passing, or climbing hills.

countersteering A counter-intuitive riding technique that allows scooters to change directions quickly. While momentarily pushing the grips left, you lean and turn to the right. This technique is imperative to learn as a rider of anything on two wheels.

cowl The protective panels that cover the engine, the spare tire, and other parts, depending on a scooter's design.

curb weight Unlike dry weight, this number refers to a vehicle full of necessary fluids and as you might find it sitting by the curb in ready-to-ride condition.

CVT A Continuously Variable Transmission commonly has two variable pulleys and a rubber drive belt. Unlike automotive automatic transmissions, a CVT has no gears.

disc brakes A metal rotor or disc spins with your wheel and a caliper clamps down on it when the brake lever is pulled. The friction between the pads and the rotor slows and stops the wheel.

displacement During a single stroke of an engine, the piston moves through a volume of space; in scooter terms it is measured in cc's, or cubic centimeters.

DMV Department of Motor Vehicles.

DOT Department of Transportation.

drive belts The belt that turns the CVT.

drum brakes On scooters, drum brakes are cable actuated. Cables are simple and fairly reliable, though they do require periodic adjustment as they stretch a bit over time.

dry weight This number is common in brochures and other sales literature about how much a scooter or motorcycle weighs. It is the weight of the scooter alone, and as the name implies, without fluids like fuel, coolant, and lubricants.

ergonomics The science of human capabilities and proper fit for everything from chairs to keyboard height to scooter seats and handlebars.

fairing Fairings are the body panels designed to control air flow and reduce drag. A well-designed faring can contribute to speed and fuel economy.

four-stroke In a four-stroke engine, the piston moves down to suck in air and fuel and then moves up to compress it. The mixture is then ignited and the piston moves down again. Finally it moves up to push all the exhaust gasses out. This adds up to four piston movements, or strokes, per combustion cycle.

fork The front suspension system of a motorcycle or scooter. In its common form it is a pair of telescoping tubes that contain shocks and springs.

friction roller drive A roller that directly acts upon the rear tire to propel the scooter forward.

FTC Federal Trade Commission.

gross weight An upper maximum weight for the vehicle, its fluids, occupants, and cargo. Going above this weight is unsafe.

half-helmet Also known as a skull cap, it only protects the skull, offering no chin or eye protection.

horsepower   This is the amount of torque an engine can produce over a given time. Horsepower plays a major role in top speed.

idle speed   How fast the engine runs when at idle. The idle speed is easily adjusted by the turn of a screw on the carburetor.

Kevlar   DuPont's aramid fiber. Kevlar has many applications, ranging from drive belts, to armor, to bullet-proof vests.

kill switch   Mounted next to the throttle for accessibility, a kill switch shuts down the engine. The U.S. Department of Transportation mandates this safety feature on all motorcycles and scooters sold in the United States.

lane sharing or **lane splitting**   Riding between cars along the white dotted line. It is legal in California and requires riders' complete focus.

legshield   The panel on the front of a scooter that your legs are behind while riding.

liquid cooled   Involves pumping a coolant through the engine and then through a radiator. The benefits typically include a more stable operating temperature and more power, while retaining or lowering the emissions of a similar air-cooled engine.

load capacity   The maximum amount of weight a scooter can safely carry.

moped   In scooter terms, it's usually a bicycle style with a small engine. In legal terms, it can be a small displacement scooter with no pedals.

open-faced helmet   Also known as a ¾ helmet, it offers no chin protection but often has an eye shield.

piston   A piston moves inside the cylinder and it transforms the expansion of a burning gas into power. The power then is used to turn the CVT, forcing the roller weights to engage and turn the rear wheel.

powerband   The range of operating speeds under which the engine is able to operate efficiently.

roller weights   Small weights that are located in the CVT and roll outward with centrifugal force when the variator begins to turn.

sidecar   A scooter sidecar is a small trailer that attaches to the side of the scooter so that it rides on three wheels. They usually can hold a passenger.

sleeper   A vehicle that appears to be unmodified with hidden performance enhancements. Typically underestimated, they are known to surprise unsuspecting victims at stoplights.

Snell Memorial Foundation   Also known as Snell for short, it sets voluntary standards for helmets.

split saddle seats   Usually on vintage scooters, a split saddle is two bicycle-style seats, one behind the other, instead of a single bench seat.

top box   A case attached to the rear of the scooter featuring lockable, and usually watertight, storage.

top speed   The fastest your scooter will go in normal conditions.

torque   The amount of raw force the engine can output. Torque is responsible for enabling you to start from a stop, and makes a difference in climbing hills. It's a force based on rotation.

trickle charge   A charger that slowly "trickles" a charge into a battery.

two-stroke   In a two-stroke engine a piston moves down once, and up once, during one combustion cycle for a grand total of two strokes.

wheel base   The distance from the center of the front wheel to the center of the rear wheel.

wheel travel   The distance the tire is able to move up and down.

windscreen   A plastic shield that diverts wind from directly hitting a rider. They can be short, medium, or tall in height. Even a very short one can change the direction of the airflow.

Index